GOD & WOMAN

DOROTHY R. PAPE

Foreword by Norah Coggan

*A fresh look at what
the New Testament says
about women.*

MOWBRAYS
LONDON · OXFORD

First published 1977 in the U.S.A. by the
Inter-Varsity Christian Fellowship

© 1976 Inter-Varsity Christian Fellowship

This edition published in the U.K.
in shortened form by
A. R. Mowbray & Co. Ltd.,
Saint Thomas House, Becket Street,
Oxford, OX1 1SJ

ISBN 0 264 665007

Printed in Great Britain by
Redwood Burn Limited
Trowbridge & Esher

Acknowledgment is made to the
following for permission to
reprint copyrighted material:
From New Testament
Commentary, I—II, Timothy
and Titus by William Hendriksen.
Copyright 1957 by William
Hendriksen and published by
Baker Book House and
used by permission. From The
Christian Family by Larry Christenson,
published and copyright 1970,
Bethany Fellowship, Inc.,
Minneapolis, Minnesota 55438 and
reprinted by permission. From
Are Women Human? by Dorothy
Sayers, published and copyright 1971,
William B. Eerdmans Publishing Co. and used
by permission. From The Ministry
of Women in the Early Church by
Jean Daniélou, published and copyright 1961,
The Faith Press Ltd., Bedfordshire, England
and used by permission.
From The Awakening by Marie Monsen,
published by A.S. Lunde & Co.,
Oslo, Norway and used by permission.
From Daktar/Diplomat in Bangladesh by
Viggo Olsen. Copyright 1973.
Moody Press, Moody Bible Institute of Chicago.
Used by permission. From The Place
of Women in the Church by Charles C. Ryrie.
Copyright 1968. Moody Press, Moody
Bible Institute of Chicago.
Used by permission.
From Pastoral Problems in First
Corinthians, by J. Stanley Glen.
Copyright © MCMLXIV, W. L. Jenkins.
Used by permission of
The Westminster Press.

To my husband Bill, who,
in a beautiful spot in the French Alps before we were married,
taught me to think through
Bible passages myself with the help of the Spirit
before turning to the human experts

CONTENTS

Introduction

This abridged British version of the original book, *In Search of God's Ideal Woman* requires some explanation of the chapters omitted, since a few references to these remain in the text. The title also indicates the reason for references to "God's Ideal Woman" which are unnecessary under the new title and format.

The nucleus of the material appeared first in a series of articles for the Woman's Page of a quarterly for Japan missionaries. It was sparked by seeing a footnote in the Amplified Old Testament stating the lady of Proverbs 31 was "God's ideal woman," (in contrast to many uncomplimentary allusions to women in that book). As a missionary, I felt this stalwart, affluent matron with a bevy of maids might not necessarily be the blueprint of God's ideal woman, especially as half a verse is devoted to her relationship to God, and twenty and a half to her physical qualities, activities, and possessions. Thus I began an exciting odessy through the New Testament, searching for every reference to woman to try to find what God really wants of us. It was an enlightening, puzzling, but rewarding experience.

Returning home in 1967 to the clarion claims of the Women's Liberation Movement, with charges and counter-charges about what Christianity has done for women, I felt an urge to enlarge my findings to book-length. Certainly Christ's attitude to women has changed every society which accepts His teachings, and while Paul didn't advocate changing the legal status of slaves and wives as property, his instructions to husbands were very revolutionary!

Unfortunately in this abridgement the last chapters on women with a ministry in the early church, and more recent missionary work, had to be cut, and more important, those on the Single woman and Widow, and woman as Wife, and as Mother. I particularly regret that on single women since it is from their ranks God has raised up and used missionaries in many areas, both to the conversion of men and women and also in "church planting" and related work. Mary Slessor and Amy Carmichael will be familiar to many in England. Founders and supporters of 'faith' missions, such as D. L. Moody, Hudson Taylor, and Fredrik Franson (who founded seven European missions, plus what is now The Evangelical Alliance Mission in North America, originally to augment Hudson Taylor's work in China) are notable for their encouragement of women's full participation in missionary ministry.

With the present rethinking, at home, of the whole question of the ministry for women in mind, I must just mention here two New Testament texts which bear on it, but which many commentators miss. In I Cor. 7 : 34-35 Paul states: "The unmarried woman careth for the things of the Lord, that she may be holy in body and spirit; but she that is married careth for the things of the world, how she may please her husband. And I speak this to your profit ... that ye may attend upon the Lord without distraction."

Ignoring here the intriguing question of whether a wife is an unholy Christian, just what are these "things of the Lord" the unmarried woman is to be occupied with? Was she to forgo the prospect of a husband and family just to dust pews or arrange flowers? In a dozen commentaries consulted, rarely is the woman mentioned, and no suggestion ever given as to what her work could or should be. Most deal with the whole paragraph in relation to the man only, many feeling sure it doesn't really mean men shouldn't marry!

I Tim. 5:9-12 is also a strange passage most church leaders ignore today. What exactly was the function of these widows? Some claim they were just indigent, needing help; but Jerome demanded they "demean themselves as becometh holiness, that their very walk, motions, countenance, language, and silence should present a certain decorous and sacred dignity." This seems rather much to require of those in need of a handout—or even to do the lowly foot-washing. Father Jean Daniélou throws light on what widows actually did in his booklet, *The Ministry of Women in the Early Church*. Most Protestants will probably be surprised at its extent before women with any spiritual interest were syphoned off into the new nunneries, and an esoteric priestcraft developed in the mediaeval church. What is the New Testament view of the ministry, now that Christ is our high priest who has offered the one perfect sacrifice for ever? What does the "priesthood of all believers" mean? May all Christians be "ambassadors for Christ" beseeching the lost to be reconciled to God?

The views and insights of this book come from knowing of God's use of women particularly in China, but also other areas, and from my own experience of Christian work in England, China, Canada, Japan, and now Germany. Writing commentaries with no knowledge of anything but centuries-old western churches full of tradition

13

is very different from bringing to birth churches in a pagan land, now, and in New Testament times. Commentators and even translators of the Bible have shown a natural and probably unconscious male bias in the past. What is needed now is a new and open-minded approach to the original documents to find all possible meanings of all references to women, rather than starting with one thing Paul said about women and ignoring, or twisting the meaning of others, to fit that one.

I'm a wife and grandmother, and firmly believe a mother's place is mainly in the home while children are there. But that period rarely lasts more than 25 years today, a third of the average life span, leaving plenty of time to serve Christ in whatever way He may indicate. 'Role' is not a Biblical term, and rather than blindly following custom and tradition, each needs to receive personal operational instructions from Christ Himself, plus His power to perform them. Only then can we qualify for that wonderful quality of relationship with Him which He promised: "Whosoever shall do the will of my Father in heaven, the same is my brother, and *sister* and mother."

DOROTHY R. PAPE

The lines along which Mrs. Pape's mind moved, as she considered the writing of this book, are most intriguing. Her verdicts on previous commentators are surely original. She says, "The writing of Bible commentaries has been a male monopoly." "Things said just about women do not seem important to male theologians. . . . Instructions dealing with her relationship to man . . . are regarded with the utmost gravity".

She began the subject by studying the ideal woman described in Proverbs and found to her surprise that she is not the docile, demure, place-is-in-the-home type that many commentators portray, but a busy executive, efficient and confident and the breadwinner of the family. This set her questioning—"is this the final blueprint of God's ideal woman"?—and so began her study of the New Testament to find the answer.

As an introduction she went to other parts of the world (and Mrs. Pape has done this in person, in England, China, Japan, Canada, and Germany have been her homes). She considered religions where 'Women, dogs and other impure animals' are classed together; where women's highest praise consisted in not being mentioned; where men thanked God daily that they were not born a woman.

Our Lord's view of women came as a great refreshment. He healed them, raised their dead, revealed new truths to them and displayed His confidence in them.

They travelled in His company. He gave the first evidence of His risen life to them.

The book goes on with studies of women in the Acts and the Epistles and struggles with problems of interpretation, of the 'covered head', of short or long or 'loosened' hair. What is an 'official' service? What kind of 'speaking' does St. Paul mean?—Is it whispering to her husband in church? Should a woman speak in front of men? "Is woman limited to being a perpetual and mute bench-warmer" (what a telling description!) "never destined to overflow with the good news of Christ"?

Women's ministry in the Epistles makes an interesting study, as does their work in the Church age, from Blandina and Perpetua, through the nineteenth century renewal and missionary revival, to active women living now.

The ordination of women, one of the pressing issues of today, is hardly mentioned, but perhaps the writer is not an Anglican. We are left however, with a thoroughly biblical and positive guide full of illustrations and with a long bibliography for further reading. The thanks of many Christian women—and men—will go to Mrs. Pape for her thoughtful and thought provoking study.

NORAH COGGAN.

30.1.78

I

WOMAN IN THE GOSPELS

1
IN CONTRAST TO OTHER RELIGIONS

To read through the four Gospels to see what they reveal about woman and, in particular, Christ's dealings with women, is rewarding and thrilling—at least for a woman. To me it brought new insights.

In general, both by word and action, the Lord portrays the fact, stated by Paul, that in Christ "there is neither male nor female" (Gal. 3:28). Occasionally, he almost seems to favor women by demonstrating special compassion, giving great praise or revealing some of the greatest New Testament truths to them; and never does he utter to them the strong rebukes he addresses to both his own disciples and the national religious leaders. Nowhere is there any statement of the inferiority of woman, nor are there any lists of do's and don'ts applying to her in particular. Indeed, the harmonious balance of the references to the two sexes in the Gospels is so permeating that few who have grown up in a Christian culture are consciously aware of it.

"Women, Dogs, and Other Impure Animals"   One of the first things that should strike us is the considerable number of contacts and conversations that Christ had with women. We are so familiar with these that we probably do not even notice them as remarkable, especially if we have no first-hand knowledge of other religions. For example, Gautama, later known as the Buddha, from the time he deserted his young wife and baby to begin his great search for Enlightenment, constantly shunned women. Although today he is credited with a great universal compassion and love for all living creatures, his attitude to women is somewhat reminiscent of Solomon's, judged by the sayings attributed to him: "Women are evil, jealous and stupid." "Avoid the sight of them." "Do not speak to them."

Gautama believed that only a celibate monastic life would enable a man to tread the difficult path to Enlightenment. He assumed that a woman's innate desire for a family would be too strong for her to endure such monasticism for long, and also that she would prove a temptation to the men who sought to follow that path. It was only after constant pleadings from the aunt who had brought him up that Gautama allowed the formation of a monastic order of nuns. This order had very restrictive rules, which included a humiliating subordination to men; for example, a nun, however old, must always stand in the presence of a monk, however young. He also prophesied, very mistakenly, that since women had come into his religion it would not last five hundred years.

In Hinduism, to be born a woman was regarded as evidence of some failure in the previous life, and, although it was an improvement on being born an insect or non-sacred animal, she still had not merited the highest state of being born a male. She was therefore merely a body for the sexual pleasure of a husband, condemned to burn on the funeral pyre if he should die first, which itself would be attributable to some omission on her part. Even when this practice of *suttee* was made illegal by the British rulers of India, at the instigation of the great evangelical social reformer Lord Shaftesbury, for a long time a widow was little more than a household drudge, perpetually disgraced.

Confucius had little to say about women except to lay down rules governing their duty to father, husband and eldest son. His disciples were men, and his teaching was mainly concerned with the state and with the character of the ruler. Women in China were treated with a little more respect than in most other Asian countries, however, and a first wife never lost her status even when others were taken to produce sons.

I have read that outside many Moslem mosques there used to be a sign, "Women, Dogs, and Other Impure Animals not Permitted." Although Mohammed seems to have respected his first wife, a wealthy widow who had originally employed him in her caravan business, in later life he obviously regarded women as existing merely for the sexual use of men. One of his own wives was a six-year-old with whom he began intercourse when she was nine. Early travelers and missionaries in Moslem lands told horrible tales of the conditions in which the women there lived. Women in these countries have rarely been accorded legal rights until recently. Just months ago women were finally allowed to enter the mosques for worship, but they may only stand at the back, behind the kneeling men.

The influence of Greek culture was still strong in Christ's

day, and although Plato had advocated equal education for women, few agreed with him. Aristotle admitted that "moral goodness is possible in every type of personage, even a woman or slave," but the general feeling of the time was that a woman's highest praise consisted in not being mentioned at all. In the light of such sentiments, Christ's frequent contacts with and references to women are all the more remarkable.

Even an orthodox Jewish man was taught to thank God daily that he was not born a woman. An American preacher once mentioned that he had recently attended an Orthodox Jewish wedding in Israel. The bride said she would introduce her grandfather, a rabbi, to him and his wife, but warned that the wife must not try to shake hands with the rabbi. In fact, when the introduction was made, the rabbi ignored her completely, speaking only to the husband. How revolutionary, then, the attitude of the Master as he moved about and taught in the Israel of his day, full of grace and truth, of courtesy and compassion, and with comprehension of the needs and capacity for spiritual insight of the women of that day and of all time.

Two Favored Women   We do have one picture of woman at her worst in the Gospels, although it is not in any association with Christ. No, I am not thinking of the woman "taken in adultery," but of Herodias and her daughter; the one out of pique demanding the head of John the Baptist, the other callously displaying it on a dish before the assembled guests. This cruel murder was more than matched, however, by Herod the Great's slaughter of the infants in Bethlehem, as well, incidentally, of his own wife and several sons—thus causing Augustus Caesar to say in a witty pun that he would rather be Herod's hog than his son.

In happy contrast to the murderous Herodias, the first women we encounter in the Gospels are the two specially favored by God with miraculous conceptions: Elizabeth, the wife of the priest Zacharias, and her young relative, Mary of Nazareth.

Some of the words used to describe Elizabeth reveal much about the feeling toward women in that day. That sad word *barren*, with its connotation of "useless, unprofitable, empty," is used to denote her (Lk. 1:7). Elizabeth herself, when sure that she was pregnant, praised God, saying, "Thus hath the Lord dealt with me . . . to take away my reproach among men" (Lk. 1:25).

Until very recently, in most parts of the world, a woman has been seen mainly as a baby-producing machine, as someone to perpetuate the family line of the father and also to carry on the worship of the ancestors. Even Martin Luther, great Christian that he was, stated, "If a woman becomes weary, or at last dead from child-bearing, that matters not; she is there to do it." For a woman not to become pregnant has usually been taken as a sign that she is displeasing to the gods and has been regarded as just grounds for divorce or the taking of a concubine. Even in modern Japan some husbands do not register their wife on the family record at the ward office until she has produced a son.

Yet Elizabeth had not been displeasing to God, for the Scripture states specifically that she and her husband "were both righteous before God, walking in all the commandments and ordinances of the Lord blameless" (Lk. 1:6). In fact, God had chosen her for the high honor of bearing a son who, "in the spirit and power of Elijah" (Lk. 1:17), was to prepare the way for the Messiah. Furthermore, he was to be "filled with the Holy Ghost, even from his mother's womb" (Lk. 1:15), so that in a very special sense Elizabeth enjoyed the presence and power of God within her.

God first gave the news of Elizabeth's pregnancy to the father, who found it hard to believe even though he had long prayed for it. Concerning Jesus' birth it was to Mary, the mother, that the announcement initially came. Surely here, in this girl chosen above every other one in all the generations of the Jewish race, we would expect to find "God's ideal woman," if there is such a thing. Yet in contrast to the bustling, brawny matron of Proverbs, we have no clue as to the kind of figure Mary had, what kind of housekeeper she was, how late or early she worked, what kind of clothes she wore. We know that she was of the royal house of David, as was Joseph, but there appears to have been no wealth left in their branches of the family, judging by the temple offering of two turtle doves after Jesus' birth.

There are a few other facts we can discover about Mary. She was a thoughtful person, as evidenced in her question to the angel, "How shall this be?" (Lk. 1:34). Then she "cast in her mind what manner of salutation" the angel had given (Lk. 1:29), and later "she kept all these things, and pondered them in her heart" (Lk. 2:19). She also had an extensive knowledge of the Scriptures, and possibly some poetic gift, for there are at least twelve Old Testament references in her famous outburst of praise known as the *Magnificat*.

At the marriage in Cana, she gave the best advice any person has ever given to another when she told the servants, "Whatsoever he saith unto you, do it" (Jn. 2:5). Perhaps it was this trait which made God see her as the best human vehicle he could find for the incredible purpose he had in mind. At any rate, the angel Gabriel was sent to her with the message, "Thou art highly favoured, the Lord is with thee! Blessed art thou among women!" (Lk. 1:28).

Mary was frankly puzzled and alarmed at this supernatural greeting. The angel hastened to tell her she had no need to fear, assuring her again she had found favor with God. Then he revealed the way in which God was going to demonstrate his approval: She was to conceive and bear a son who was to be called *Jesus*. "He shall be great, and shall be called the Son of the Highest: and the Lord God shall give unto him the throne of his father David: and he shall reign over the house of Jacob for ever, and of his kingdom there shall be no end" (Lk. 1:32-33).

Mary's response was not immediate, ecstatic joy at this news, which some authorities tell us every Jewish maiden hoped for. "How shall this be, seeing I know not a man?" she asked (Lk. 1:34). This seems rather strange since Mary was already betrothed to Joseph. However, the footnotes to Luke's Gospel in the *Cambridge Greek Testament* series quote one view that "an *immediate* conception is the idea conveyed by the Hebrew source underlying Luke's Greek, and Mary's question is natural, and not incredulity but surprise," since she was not yet married.

At any rate, Mary was not reproved for scepticism, as was Zacharias when he doubted the ability of his wife to conceive in old age. Instead, with inimitable delicacy of description Mary was given details of how she was to become the mother of this Holy Son of the eternal God Almighty: "The Holy Ghost shall come upon thee, and the power of the Highest shall overshadow thee: therefore also that which shall be born of thee shall be called the Son of God" (Lk. 1:35).

The Buddha, Princess Blooming-Tree-Blossom and the Sky-Kami The annotator of the above-mentioned Greek version of Luke's Gospel dismisses this whole narrative as having "little historical foundation ... entirely character-istic of the naive supernaturalism of primitive and popular thought, completely uncritical towards wonders." Surely he must see that neither Zacharias nor Mary was naively cre-dulous and that there is something in the wording of the explanation given Mary which is of a far different quality than the birth legends of other great religious figures.

Of the Buddha, legends not written until several cen-turies after his death variously claim that in a previous existence he was a bird and an animal and that his mother dreamed that a small white elephant entered her side. When the time of the birth arrived, she stood upright, sup-porting herself with the branch of a fig tree while, accord-ing to one account, a god gathered up in a sheet the child of her womb. Another version has some of the gods re-ceiving him in a golden net and worshiping him—where-upon the baby surveyed the ten quarters of the world, took seven steps across it and cried in the voice of a lion: "I am the chief in the world. This is my last birth. There is now no existence again."

The *Kojiki* and *Nihonji,* translated together as *The Sacred Scriptures of the Japanese,* carry the story of how a sky deity, grandson of the supreme Sun Goddess, mated with a human, Princess Blooming-Tree-Blossom, with equally bizarre details.

A Comforting Visit   Let us return now to Mary's meeting with the angel. After revealing how she was to become the mother of the Son of God, he gave her an added assurance of God's power by telling her that her elderly relative Eliza-beth was already six months pregnant; "for with God noth-ing shall be impossible" (Lk. 1:37).

Following this encouraging declaration, Mary's response, I think we can assume, is typical of one whom God looks upon with favor, "Behold the handmaid of the Lord; be it unto me according to thy word" (Lk. 1:38). The full force of this is wonderfully expressed in J. B. Phillips' version: 'I belong to the Lord, body and soul,' replied Mary, 'let it happen as you say.' "

What a practical comfort and strengthening of faith it must have been to Mary to be able to confer with another woman who had also had a remarkable visitation from God and a miraculous conception. Without delay, Mary hurried off and traveled, apparently alone, the nearly one hundred miles to see Elizabeth.

The greeting she received must have been full of sweet assurance that it was no fanciful vision she had seen, but a true messenger of God. Elizabeth felt the child within her stir excitedly as Mary entered. Filled with the Holy Spirit, the older woman cried out,

Blessed are you among women, and blessed is your child! What an honor it is to have the mother of my Lord come to see me! Why, as soon as your greeting reached my ears, the child within me jumped for joy! Oh, how happy is the woman who believes in God, for He does make His promises to her come true. (Lk. 1:42-45, Phillips)

Then comes that famous song which some commentators consider so brilliant it must have been composed by Luke—obviously too good for a woman! Another commentator suggests it was a messianic psalm that might have been used by any Jew of the period. Three Old Latin manuscripts have the song coming from Elizabeth's lips. For the most part it is equally appropriate for both women, but the promise to "Abraham and his seed for ever" seems to refer to the coming of the Messiah and therefore would be more fitting coming from Mary.

Mary stayed with Elizabeth three months, possibly

through the trials of morning sickness, then returned for the inevitable revelation of her pregnancy to her family and fiancé. But once again God smoothed the way by appearing to Joseph, while he was planning for a separation, and telling him that it was the Holy Spirit who had made Mary the mother of a son who was to be the Savior from sin (Mt. 1: 19-23). The angel added that this was to be the fulfillment of a prophecy of Isaiah: "Behold, a virgin shall be with child, and shall bring forth a son."

So we find angel messengers from God appearing to both Zacharias and Elizabeth, to both Mary and Joseph. When the infant Jesus was taken to Jerusalem for the purification rite, he was publicly recognized and blessed both by the old man Simeon and the old prophetess Anna. From then on the harmonious balancing of the references to both men and women throughout the Gospel records continues to be impressive.

2
IN THE CONTENT OF CHRIST'S TEACHINGS

The complementary references to the sexes noted in the previous chapter, and particularly evident in the details of Christ's birth, are observable also in the content and pattern of Christ's teaching. For example, after performing some miracles in Galilee, he returned home to begin his public ministry in Nazareth; and in his first discourse he used as illustrations the Gentile widow who had cared for Elijah and the Gentile general, Naaman, who was healed of leprosy by Elisha (Lk. 4:25-27).

We read of a certain woman, crippled for eighteen years, whom Christ healed on the Sabbath in a synagogue. He evidently noted her in the women's gallery, called her down beside him and actually touched her, bringing immediate healing. In response, she "glorified God," presumably in an audible voice. When the ruler of the synagogue remonstrated at this double breach of law and custom, Christ answered, "You hypocrites; every single one of you unties his ox or his ass . . . on the Sabbath and leads him away to water. This woman, a *daughter of Abraham* . . . should be released from her bonds on the Sabbath" (Lk. 13:10-17, Phillips). Christ gave the woman a title of honor, not merely indicating that she was of more value than an animal but also emphasizing her spiritual status and privilege as a daughter of Abraham, the father of the Jewish race.

On another Sabbath, when he healed a man with dropsy and was again criticized, he merely answered, "Which of you shall have an ass or ox fallen into a pit, and will not straightway pull him out on the sabbath day?" (Lk. 14:5). Yet on the previous occasion he had taken the trouble to emphasize the woman's worth and spiritual status.

Christ raised from the dead young people of each sex, largely, it seems, out of compassion for the parents. These were the only son of the widow of Nain (Lk. 7:12-16) and the only daughter of Jairus, the ruler of a synagogue (Lk. 8:41-42, 49-56).

When some unbelieving Jews came demanding a sign from heaven, the Lord used both a male and a female illustration to drive home his point. He rebuked these Jews for not believing the evidence of what he had done already by saying that the men of Nineveh, who had believed Jonah's message and repented, would judge them for their unbelief. He added that the Queen of the South would rise up in judgment against them, for she had gone on a long journey to hear the wisdom of Solomon, while they had a greater than Solomon in their very midst (Lk. 11:29-32).

In his teaching about the kingdom of God, Christ used illustrations referring to both sexes. To explain the nature of the kingdom, he said it is like a man planting mustard seed in his garden and like a woman mixing yeast in her flour to make bread (Lk. 13:19-21). He also included what he knew they would regard as the worst of both sexes when he told the religious leaders that publicans and harlots would enter the kingdom of God before them (Mt. 21:31). To reveal his great concern for each individual member of lost humanity, Christ told the stories of a shepherd looking in dangerous places for his one lost sheep and a woman searching and sweeping every nook and corner of her house for her one lost coin (Lk. 15:3-10).

Among the parables illustrating different aspects of prayer is one about a woman who finally got an unjust judge to act on her behalf simply because she persisted in asking him until he was sick of the sight of her. This is followed by the story of two men who went into the temple to pray. One, a Pharisee, prayed only "with himself "; the other, a publican, prayed a penitential prayer to God (Lk. 18:1-14).

In warning people to be ready for his second coming, Jesus used a parable about men to whom various amounts of money were given to use until their master's return and a parable about ten virgins, half of whom were not prepared for the coming of the bridegroom (Mt. 25). When explaining the suddenness of his coming, he stated that two men would be working in a field and one would be taken, the other left; two women would be grinding at a mill, with the same result (Mt. 24:40-41).

The Male and Female Principle in the Godhead   In contrast to this wealth of material touching on women in Christ's teaching, I have recently read a book on a certain Hindu sect which has only three references to women in its 191 pages—and these are only incidental to the teachings. One, for example, is about a young disciple who had been sent for training to a famous guru. When he arrived and was invited into the house, he saw the guru place his hand on his wife's shoulder in an affectionate way. It was considered very improper in India to perform such an action before others, and the young man was shaken, wondering how he could learn anything of an advanced spiritual nature from such a person. But just as he was about to leave in disgust, the guru removed his hand from his wife's shoulder and put it in the blazing fire! From this the disciple was said to have learned the truth of "nonpreferential discrimination," or that there is no distinction between Brahman's various manifestations.

While many religions have had both male and female deities, the latter have often been in the role of consorts to the gods; and all the gods are usually portrayed with various human failings such as jealousy, pride, lust. In the holy character of the creator God of the Bible there is a wonderful blend of the ideal characteristics of both father and mother. In the Old Testament Isaiah gives us a picture of the latter: "Can a woman forget her sucking child, that she should not have compassion on the son of her womb? Yea, they may forget, yet will I not forget thee" (Is. 49:15). A nursing mother may manage to forget a child for three or four hours or during a night's sleep before the discomfort of the unused milk supply brings remembrance, if not compassion. But God in his love does not forget his own for a moment; he neither slumbers nor sleeps. We also have a simile of motherhood in Isaiah 66:13: "As one whom his mother comforteth, so will I comfort you."

On the other hand, Christ often stressed the father nature of God and taught the disciples to use that name in prayer. He usually referred to himself as Son of Man. He once stated, though, that "the hairs of your head are all numbered" in God's sight, and, to me at least, this conjures up a picture of a mother lovingly brushing her child's hair each day, knowing so well each differing glint in color, each wayward curl or awkward cowlick. The co-creator of the universe also once attributed a mother's instinct to himself when he said, "O Jerusalem, Jerusalem... how often would I have gathered thy children together, even as a hen gathereth her chickens under her wings" (Mt. 23:37).

It is true that we see both the male and female principles attributed to the powerful forces of nature by most animist religions. This is perhaps most evident in the well-known Chinese Taoist teaching of the *Yin* and the *Yang*. In the China section of *Religions in a Changing World* we read, *There is the* Yin, *which stands for earth, the moon, darkness, evil, and the female sex. On the other hand is the* Yang, *which includes Heaven, the sun, light, fire, goodness, and the male sex. The gods (Shen) are also associated with the* Yang *and therefore are in opposition to the evil spirits (Kuei) which are* Yin.

How different are these characteristics from Christ's teaching of a loving, personal God where the father/mother qualities are not opposed or in conflict but complementary and harmonious!

The Sexless Element in Christ's Teachings Christ teachings also contain an element which we might call *sexless*. Nowhere do we find Christ giving instructions to women as women, that is, nowhere does he give commands applicable to women only. He did not tell Martha and Mary they ought to be married. He did not rebuke the mothers present at the feeding of the four thousand for being away from home three days listening to theology. He did not give any directions about housekeeping or about women's place in the synagogue.

Even in his instructions to the disciples, there are few which obviously apply to men alone. The only ones I noticed were "Whosoever looketh on a woman to lust after her hath committed adultery with her already in his heart" (Mt. 5:28); "Whosoever shall put away his wife, saving for the cause of fornication, causeth her to commit adultery" (Mt. 5:32); and "Be not ye called Rabbi, for one is your Master, even Christ; and all ye are brethren" (Mt. 23:8).

It is noteworthy, too, that the things on which Christ said those who claim him as Lord will finally be judged—feeding the hungry, clothing the naked, visiting the sick and prisoners—are things which mostly can and should be done equally by men and women (Mt. 25:31-46).

When the Sadducees came with their story of a woman given to seven brothers in succession and asked whose wife she would be in the resurrection, Christ explained that in heaven there will be no marriage, but we shall be as "the angels of God" (Mt. 22:30), who presumably are unisex or, rather, non-sexed. Thus it seems our sexuality will be forgotten, our chief delight being to see Christ's face and to serve him.

Finally, we cannot help noticing that in a few instances Christ seems to have taken special care to include women in his teaching. In Mark 7:10-11, when speaking about honoring parents, he repeats *father* and *mother* four times in two verses. At first I wondered if there was no word for "parents" in Greek, but later found a number of statements in the Gospels which include that word. So he seems to be emphasizing that both father and mother are to be honored equally, in contrast to current Rabbinic teaching.

When speaking of the cost of discipleship, he also included the female members of families as being affected. "Suppose ye that I am come to give peace on earth? I tell you, Nay; but rather division. . . . The father shall be divided against the son, and the son against the father; the mother against the daughter, and the daughter against the mother; the mother-in-law against her daughter-in-law" (Lk. 12:51, 53). Again, "There is no man that hath left house, or brethren, or sisters, or father, or mother, or wife, or children . . . for my sake, and the gospel's, but he shall receive an hundredfold . . . houses, and brethren, and sisters, and mothers, and children" (Mk. 10:29-30).

Another memorable occasion when Christ deliberately added the female element is recorded by both Matthew and Mark. He was speaking to a large crowd, evidently in a house, when his mother and brothers came looking for him. "Then one said unto him, Behold, thy mother and thy brethren stand without, desiring to speak with thee. But he answered, and said unto him, Who is my mother? and who are my brethren? And he stretched forth his hand toward his disciples, and said, Behold my mother and my brethren! For whosoever shall do the will of my Father . . . the same is my brother, *and sister* and mother" (Mt. 12:46-50; Mk. 3:31-35).

We do not know why he took the trouble to add that *sister,* but surely we have here part of the blueprint for God's ideal person—woman or man, young or old, married or single. They are the ones who do his will.

3
WOMEN IN CHRIST'S COMPANY

Christ did not call a woman to be among the twelve apostles chosen at the beginning of his public ministry to forsake their work and go with him everywhere. To have called a single woman would obviously have led to unsavory suspicions, while most married women were presumably busy taking care of their families. It is remarkable, therefore, that we later do find women traveling in his company.

The majority of us would agree, I think, that men are generally more qualified for such responsibilities. From a physical point of view alone, their voices are stronger and so more suited for preaching, particularly before the days of amplifiers. They are also free from the time-demanding work of bearing and rearing children. Further, many have objective, analytical minds, able to isolate the principles of theology or whatever. Perhaps the majority of women tend to be more interested in people than concepts, and, while this can be a real advantage in Christian work, it may sometimes degenerate into personality conflicts intensified by gossip, although these are certainly not limited to one sex.

It is noteworthy, however, that the Gospels record two occasions where Christ defended women's intuition against the reasoning of the Twelve. When some women brought their children to Jesus to be blessed, the disciples rebuked them and tried to shoo them away. At that, Jesus was "much displeased, and said unto them, Suffer the little children to come unto me, and forbid them not: for of such is the kingdom of God" (Mk. 10:14). When Mary of Bethany poured costly ointment on Jesus' head, the disciples were indignant at this "waste." The Lord said then that this woman's act would be told as a memorial to her wherever the gospel would be preached—as indeed it has. In contrast, there are a few of the Twelve, whom we generally suppose to be the most important church leaders, about whom the Scripture gives no detail and to whom it gives no commendation.

Female Volunteers Considering the cultural context and the practical problems, it is all the more surprising to read that women were added to his company for an unspecified length of time:

It came to pass afterward, that he went throughout every city and village, preaching and shewing the glad tidings of the kingdom of God: and the twelve were with him. And certain women, which had been healed of evil spirits and infirmities, Mary called Magdalene, out of whom went seven devils, and Joanna the wife of Chuza, Herod's steward, and Susanna, and many others, which ministered unto him of their substance. (Lk. 8:1-3)

Some of these women, at least, were married, and one cannot help wondering how they were free to leave home and how they had money to contribute, when legally they were not independent persons. At any rate, it is good to know that there were some women willing to endure the discomfort of travel and uncertain lodging places in their efforts to minister to Christ and his disciples. Their liberality and gratitude seem a little different from the attitude of the Twelve, who, although they had initially left all to follow the Master, were very interested in what they would gain in return. Even when he had just told them of his imminent crucifixion, they were only concerned, apparently, with the most important seats in the kingdom.

It may well be justifiable to assume, as many have, that because Christ did not choose any women among the Twelve, there should be no women leaders in the Christian church. This book is certainly not meant as a brief for women ministers. However, it could be pointed out that he did not choose a Gentile either. In fact, he did not institute anything resembling most churches today, with one pastor trained in an academic seminary, Sunday schools and other things we now consider good and useful.

Furthermore, after the apostles replaced Judas by drawing lots (Acts 1:15-26), there seems to have been no later effort to perpetuate a ruling hierarchy of twelve men. Actually, Christ had promised the original apostles that "in the regeneration when the Son of man shall sit in the throne of his glory, ye also shall sit upon twelve thrones, judging the twelve tribes of Israel" (Mt. 19:28). Thus he seems to have ignored the whole future structure of the Christian church, only telling his disciples they were not to be like the Gentiles, lording it over others.

Whether Christ did not call a woman to be one of the Twelve out of consideration for the difficulties it might raise or out of a feeling that it would be wrong to have a woman in such a position, we are not told. But he certainly did not object to their voluntarily joining themselves to his company.

Ever since these first women traveled with Christ, women have usually comprised the majority of any Christian congregation. No one who is not a woman can appreciate the sense of hope, comfort, understanding and inspiration a woman receives from studying Christ in the Gospels. And for those who were able to meet him on earth the effect must have been doubled. Nowhere does Christ use the words *subordinate* or *subject* in connection with women. He does not compare them on a superior/inferior basis with men. His words, "Take my yoke upon you, and learn of me; for I am meek and lowly in heart" (Mt. 11:29), seem so eminently right, an invitation we want to respond to in our best moments; and this invitation was apparently offered to all who were listening, men and women alike.

Shocking Words from Uninspired Commentators   When we turn from the inspired words of the Gospels to those of some commentators, we receive an unpleasant shock. I made my original study of the Gospels in Japan without consulting any commentaries and found it a tremendous inspiration and encouragement. Since being home, however, I have read other views, some which follow odd tangents from the base of the scriptural record.

Walter F. Adeney, for example, in *Women of the New Testament* states, "Our Lord's relations with the women who attended Him are distinct from His relations with men disciples in one very remarkable particular. He ministered to men; but women ministered to Him. In their case Jesus consented to receive gifts and service."

This idea is hard to substantiate from Scripture. Christ

did not minister only to men. He healed both men and women. He provided wine for all the wedding guests at Cana and fed the five-thousand and the four-thousand men plus many women and children. Nor do we find only women ministering to Christ. After a boy provided the loaves and fishes to feed the multitude, the disciples served everyone. A man with a pitcher donated the use of his upper room where Peter and John, not women, prepared the Passover Feast. Both Matthew and Zaccheus ministered to Christ by providing hospitality.

It does not appear that Christ did not *want* men to do any ministering, but rather that some of them were often too proud and thoughtless to serve. "One of the Pharisees" also held a feast for him, where the "woman who was a sinner" came with expensive ointment (Lk. 7:36-50). Jesus pointed out how the host, a man, had failed to show common courtesy, providing no water for his feet, no kiss of greeting, no anointing oil. At the Last Supper none of the Twelve offered to do the slave or housewife's job of washing feet. The fact that Christ "took a towel and girded himself " (Jn. 13:4) has surely been an encouragement to countless women as they have donned aprons to perform menial and unpleasant tasks. But it was given as an example to the *male* leaders of what they should be doing.

Charles C. Ryrie, in *The Place of Women in the Church*, also enlarges on the idea of women ministering to Christ: *In the life of our Lord, women had a special place as ministers to Him. This ministry consisted in caring for His physical wants by hospitality, by giving of money, and preparing spices for His dead body.* In response to this *Jesus allowed women to follow Him, He taught them, and He honored them with the first announcement of His resurrection. But equally important, He limited their activity by not choosing one of them for official work. Thus we may*

41

say that, while Jesus granted great freedom to women, and placed importance on their ministrations, He limited the sphere of their activity by glorifying the domestic responsibilities with which they ministered to Him. (emphasis added)

Yet Luke 8 does not say that Christ let the women follow him *in response* to being ministered to by them. Evidently, it was he who made the first move. "Certain women, which had been healed of evil spirits and infirmities, . . . ministered unto him of their substance." It seems that they loved and served him because he first graciously met their great needs. Peter's mother-in-law, too, was first healed by Christ, then ministered to him and the disciples. The idea of Christ only teaching women or allowing them to follow him after they fed him or gave him money seems utterly foreign to his character and reminds one more of the Buddha. When women continually pestered him to be allowed to follow him, he grudgingly gave in and allowed them to join his religion and to fill the monks' begging bowls with food every day.

The last part of Ryrie's statement also is questionable: "[Christ] limited their activity by not choosing one of them for official work. . . . He limited the sphere of their activity by glorifying the domestic responsibilities with which they ministered to Him." We agree, of course, that Christ did not call a woman to be one of the Twelve. But what exactly is "official work"? One preacher I heard suggested that Christ chose the Twelve for two purposes only, "that they might be with him, and that he might send them forth to preach" (Mk. 3:14). If so, Luke 8 states that the women were with Christ and the Twelve. And other passages mention women whom Christ sent with important messages, though granted these were not sermons. The woman of Samaria went to tell her village about Jesus, with the result that many believed in him. Mary and others were told to relay the glorious news of the resurrection. The woman with the issue of blood was required to make a public testimony to the crowd. At Christ's birth the prophetess Anna did quite a bit of speaking to those looking for the coming of the Messiah. We are also told she spent all her time at the temple, fasting and praying, instead of being occupied with housework (Lk. 2:36-38). While the activities of these women may not be considered "official work," they can hardly be classed as "domestic responsibilities" either.

And where in the Gospels does Christ especially "glorify" domestic work? The woman mixing bread does not seem any more "glorified" than the farmer sowing seed or dressing vines. During his visit to Bethany, when Martha was fretting about Mary's not helping her serve, Jesus said Mary's listening to him was the "good part" (Lk. 10:42). Also, he said we should not spend much thought on food and clothes, things usually regarded as domestic concerns.

I have no objection to saying that Christ glorified work, but there is no conclusive evidence in the Gospels that he only glorified *women's* work and limited their responsibilities to domestic affairs. To me, he glorified domestic chores by his own gracious interest and participation in them, providing wine for the awkward predicament at the Cana marriage feast, feeding the hungry multitudes, girding himself with a towel to wash the disciples' feet.

As we women face routine, sometimes dirty, household tasks, or when our family is at its most demanding stage, leaving us not a moment to ourselves, what a help it is to be reminded of his invitation to "Take my yoke upon you." If we do so, we will often find that much of the burden is eased from our shoulders onto his.

Finally, we have that priceless example of his "domestic"

concern and provision at the end of John's Gospel. The discouraged disciples had returned to fishing and after a fruitless night of toil wearily pulled to shore. There they found that the Lord, with the tender concern of a wife or mother, had a cheerful fire burning, breakfast cooking and an invitation to "Come and eat!" Who had fixed the fire of dirty charcoal and gutted the slippery fish? The risen Lord of Lords, with hands so brutally torn with hammer and nails, who to the very end proved that he came "not to be ministered unto, but to minister."

To such a Lord women have always been drawn, and later we shall find them bravely continuing in his company right through the long hours of the crucifixion, and beyond.

4
CHRIST'S COURTESY TO WOMEN

Having looked at women in general both in Christ's teaching and in his company, we come now to some of the most inspiring parts of the Gospels: Christ's contacts and conversations with individual women during his ministry on earth. Here again, I found some of my own discoveries and conclusions differed from some of the commentators'.

What is unique and revolutionary about Christ's attitude to women is his obvious concern and appreciation for them as *individuals*; not only did he deign to speak to them, but he actually revealed to them new spiritual truths. This is usually the most striking aspect for a woman, and also a cause of surprise for most men brought up in pagan lands. These contacts of the Lord with individual women we will try to look at with an unprejudiced mind, although granted, with a feminine eye.

Was Jesus Ever Discourteous to Women? One characteristic of Christ which amazes people from non-Christian cultures is his almost invariable courtesy to women. There are a few possible exceptions to this, the first two, surprisingly enough, involving his mother.

At the age of twelve, Jesus was taken to the Passover Feast at Jerusalem. At the end of the first day of the return journey Joseph and Mary could not find him with any of their party, so they returned to the city and finally discovered him with religious leaders in the temple. His mother began to rebuke him, saying, "Son, why hast thou thus dealt with us? Behold, thy father and I have sought thee sorrowing" (Lk. 2:48).

In any one else of that age his answer would seem precocious or even impudent: "How is it that ye sought me? Know ye not that I must be about my Father's business?" It was in fact a gentle rebuke to Mary, who had referred to Joseph as his father, indicating she may have lost the sense of Jesus' divine origin. Perhaps, as quite often happens, the daily care of a home and several small children had blunted her spiritual appetite and perception. She and Joseph seem to have been remiss in not checking earlier in the day to be sure that Jesus was with the party; however, this may just indicate their complete confidence in him.

Some commentators take the view that any special worth or greatness in Mary was merely due to her relationship as mother of Christ, emphasizing "the blessing of motherhood." Ryrie states that the lessons learned from her are "mostly related to the home," which leads one to the conclusion that Mary is significant as "a model of ideal Christian womanhood." He admits there is a dearth of material about her, but quotes James Hastings as giving the true explanation of this: "This slightness of texture is itself a note of genuine portraiture, for the reason that Mary was of a retiring nature, unobtrusive, reticent, perhaps even shrinking from observation, so that the impress of her personality was confined to the sweet sanctities of the home circle. . . . We see in the little that is told of her what a true woman ought to be."

Mary may well have been retiring and home-loving, but, with the possible exception of the angel's announcement of the coming conception, the scriptural record never shows us Mary at home. She is hurrying off to Elizabeth, then going to Bethlehem for the census, then to Jerusalem for purification rites, down to Egypt, back to Nazareth, then to Jerusalem again for the Passover, to Cana for the wedding, to Capernaum, to a city near the Sea of Galilee with her other sons to persuade Jesus to come home, and finally to Jerusalem again. It therefore requires an exercise of imagination to learn from her lessons "mostly related to the home."

While some see Mary as obtaining status and being a model of Christian womanhood only in her role of mother, I cannot help wondering if she may not have been of greater spiritual stature as a young single woman since God chose her at that time for the highest honor of nurturing within her body the very Son of God.

The second occasion when Jesus appeared to speak with a lack of courtesy to his mother was at the wedding at Cana, when she told him the bridegroom had run out of wine. His reply was, "Woman, what have I to do with thee? Mine hour is not yet come" (Jn. 2:4).

This is certainly a puzzling statement. A teacher, the head of the English department of the Chinese high school in Tokyo, once showed me this verse, which he had recently found in an English New Testament, and asked me how

47

Christ could possibly say such a thing to his mother. Both this teacher's Confucian background, with its strong emphasis on respect for parents, and his Roman Catholic faith, with its veneration of Mary, made the words repugnant to him.

There seems to be general agreement that (contrary to modern English usage) the term *Woman* was not disrespectful. And the fact that Christ used it again from the cross, instead of addressing Mary as *Mother,* suggests that his main purpose was to demonstrate that Mary could no longer hold a special relationship to him. Thus he removed any legitimate ground for Mariolatry, for adoring Mary as "Mother of God."

It is the remainder of Christ's reply which is more puzzling: "What have I to do with thee? Mine hour is not yet come." One man thinks this shows that the actions of the Son of God, after he had begun his divine work, were no longer dependent on the suggestion of a woman. (But might we not equally well add, of a man either?) Since he soon did what Mary was hoping for, it is still hard to know why he said his hour had not come. Mary, however, did not seem in the least offended, or silenced, for she turned to the servants and uttered the wisest advice ever given to any man or woman: "Whatsoever he saith unto you, do it" (Jn. 2:5).

The other possible exception to Christ's invariable courtesy to women was his conversation with the Gentile woman who begged for her daughter to be healed (Mt. 15:21-28). But the language experts tell us this was probably a witty play on words in which the woman joined. If he were only "Son of David," then she must remain a Gentile "dog"; but the latter word could also refer to a domestic pet who already had a place within the "Lord's" house. The exchange ended with Christ's high commendation, "O woman, great is thy faith."

Even when the mother of James and John, right after Christ had told them of his coming crucifixion, came with the selfish and presumptuous request that her two sons be allowed to sit on his right and left hands in his kingdom, he did not rebuke her. It was a natural ambition for a mother, and she did have a real belief that Christ was the Son of God, as far as we can judge. He merely replied, "Ye know not what ye ask. . . . To sit on my right hand, and on my left, is not mine to give, but it shall be given to them for whom it is prepared of my Father" (Mt. 20:20-23).

Three Adulteresses   To many people, men and women, the most surprising instances of Christ's courtesy are his interviews with adulteresses. Let us look first at the story in John 8:2-11. Many consider that this account is "poorly attested," in that it is omitted from a number of early manuscripts. But the incident is so superbly characteristic of Christ that it is hard to imagine any human mind concocting it. It would seem far more plausible, knowing how sex came to be regarded as evil in the Roman church, to assume that some over-prudish early Fathers feared it might encourage people in adultery and therefore omitted it from the record.

Jesus was teaching in the temple courtyard when some of the scribes and Pharisees came along dragging a woman. John tells us plainly what their motive was: to have something of which they might legitimately accuse Jesus. They set the woman in the midst of the circle of those listening to Christ and said, "Master, this woman was taken in adultery, in the very act. Now Moses in the law commanded us, that such should be stoned: but what sayest thou?"

Then came that tantalizing moment which it is hard to believe any human mind fabricated: "Jesus stooped down, and with his finger wrote on the ground." What did he write? I think an ordinary author would have told us. I have wondered if he wrote the words of Leviticus 20:10: "The man that committeth adultery with another man's wife, even he . . . the adulterer and the adulteress shall surely be put to death."

The woman's accusers continued to press him for an answer. So he stood up and uttered that amazing sentence which only the sinless Christ could have thought of saying, "He that is without sin among you, let him first cast a stone at her."

Then he continued writing. Did he write, "Whosoever looketh on a woman to lust after her hath committed adultery already in his heart?" Perhaps he merely wrote, "Where is the man?" These religious leaders claimed they had caught this woman "in the very act" of adultery, so obviously there had been a man present. Yet they in their injustice and hypocrisy had merely brought the woman, although the law of Moses had specified both the man and woman were to be killed. (This law, by the way, appears not to have been enforced in Israel for many centuries.)

In Ryrie's opinion, Christ "used this woman to teach some religious leaders the grace of forgiveness in mixing mercy with law." Surely this was not a matter of merely "using" her—a rather unpleasant term these days. Rather, he used the *occasion*, engineered by the evil intention of the religious leaders, to turn the tables on them and reveal their own injustice and hypocrisy.

John states that they "being convicted by their own conscience, went out one by one, beginning at the eldest, even unto the least." What a crestfallen procession! If they had

50

merely been learning a lesson in mercy, this action would have been quite uncalled for.

Then Jesus stood up and spoke to the woman. If he had just wanted to "use" her as an object lesson, there would have been no need for further conversation after the religious leaders left. But he was concerned for her as a person. Instead of ignoring her now, as any rabbi would have done, he spoke those inimitable words of comfort and uplift, yet words which did not overlook her failure. "Woman, where are those thine accusers? Hath no man condemned thee?" Jesus asked. And when she replied, "No man, Lord," Jesus said, "Neither do I condemn thee: go, and sin no more."

These words, which so often stick in the gullets of the self-righteous, are like healing balm to anyone who has become conscious of sin in any form in his or her life.

Another woman, this one a locally recognized "sinner" so probably a prostitute, came to Jesus at a feast, carrying an alabaster box of very expensive ointment:

[She] stood at his feet behind him weeping, and began to wash his feet with tears, and did wipe them with the hairs of her head, and kissed his feet, and anointed them with the ointment. Now when the Pharisee which had bidden him saw it, he spake within himself, saying, This man, if he were a prophet, would have known who and what manner of woman this is that toucheth him: for she is a sinner. (Lk. 7:38-39)

Jesus knew what this man was thinking, and, after telling the story of the creditor who forgave two debtors, the one owing five hundred denarii, the other fifty, he asked his host which of the two debtors would be most grateful. Simon said he supposed it would be the one who was forgiven most. Then Jesus turned toward the woman and spoke a truth which has been evident down through the centuries in the Christian church: "Her sins, which are many, are forgiven; for she loved much: but to whom little is forgiven, the same loveth little." He concluded with a word for the woman herself, again one of comfort, renewal and hope: "Thy faith hath saved thee; go in peace."

The last of this trio of stories concerns the woman at the well (Jn. 4: 5-30). Some have dubbed her "the Samaritan harlot," yet Christ said distinctly that she had had five husbands and was now evidently living in an adulterous common-law situation—which is rather different from being a professional prostitute. It would probably have been easy to guess the life of a prostitute, but both the woman and the townspeople considered it remarkable that Jesus could know this woman's unusual and colorful, though probably very sad, past. (Incidentally, I find the word *harlot* comes very easy to the commentators, whereas Christ never used this word to refer to a particular woman. His only references to such were when he told the religious leaders that the publicans and harlots who believed John's message would enter the kingdom of heaven before them.)

Alfred Edersheim, in his *Life and Times of Jesus the Messiah,* grinds this woman into the dust from a different direction, with equally little justification, it seems to me. He refers to her as the "poor, ignorant Samaritan woman," "ignorant Samaritaness of the lower order," "humble, ignorant Samaritaness," and "the ignorant woman of Sychar." He further states, "Those who know how difficult it is to lodge any new idea in the mind of uneducated rustics in this country will understand how utterly at a loss this Samaritan countrywoman must have been to grasp the meaning of Jesus."

(By "this country" Edersheim is referring to England in the 1880s, and one cannot help sympathizing with its "rustics' " difficulty in understanding Edersheim, in view of his sometimes painfully tedious erudition. One of his sentences describing the situation at Sychar's well contains 118 words, and another 129!)

But to continue:

Verse 15 [of John 4] marked the utmost limit of the woman's comprehension. We can scarcely form an adequate notion of the narrowness of such a mental horizon as her's. This accounts for His speaking to her about His own Messiahship and the worship of the future in words far more plain than He used to His own disciples. None but the plainest statements could she grasp. . . . It is not unnatural to suppose that having reached the utmost limits of which she was capable, the Saviour now asked for her husband in order that . . . the horizon might be enlarged. This is also substantially the view of some of the Fathers.

How did the early Fathers come to this view? It is hard to think of any other than a bias toward masculine superiority.

I might have thought my own view was similarly biased had I not obtained it, I believe, from a male Bible teacher. Also, I have found that Paul Little in *How to Give Away Your Faith* has the same view, namely, that Christ's conversation with the Samaritan is a superb example of how to witness graciously to *anyone* about his or her need of a Savior. Certainly Little does not regard it as geared to the limitations of a grossly ignorant countrywoman.

In fact, there is little evidence in Scripture of stupidity on this woman's part. She at once recognized Jesus as a Jew, either by his dress or by the few words of his first short request, and she was surprised that he was not putting up the usual racial and sexual barriers. Neither was she ignorant of her country's history and religion.

Her question, "Sir, thou hast nothing to draw with, and the well is deep; from whence then hast thou that living water?" seems on a par with the learned Nicodemus' question: "How can a man be born when he is old? Can he enter the second time into his mother's womb?" (Jn. 3:4). Both failed to grasp the spiritual while concerned about the material aspect of what Christ had said. There seems to be an equal mixture of plain speaking and spiritual symbolism in Christ's discourses with both these individuals. But while the woman was gradually enlightened and ended up witnessing so that many in her village believed in Christ, Nicodemus evidently had to think things through a long time, to weigh whether the praises of men and a place in the Sanhedrin were worth more than a spiritual rebirth.

Unlike Edersheim, who believed that Christ told the woman to call her husband because she was too stupid to understand Christ's words by herself, Paul Little thinks his purpose was to cause her to face the fact of her own sin without being condemned by him. "Most of us," Little states, "are quick to condemn. Often we have the mistaken idea that if we do not condemn a certain attitude or deed, we will be condoning it. But this was not our Lord's opinion."

Edersheim rejected this view on the ground that the woman does not *say* she feels convicted, but rather goes on to talk about where worship of God should take place. Yet surely most of us have experienced within ourselves, or in dealing with other people, the tendency to turn to generalizations or questions to which there is no obvious answer, rather than face up to some personal sin or shortcoming. It is a common defense mechanism.

Christ gently brought the woman back to the main issue of not *where* but *how* God is to be worshiped. It is in spirit and in truth, by men and women, whether Jew, Gentile or half-breed Samaritan, who have drunk of that water of life which only the Messiah himself can impart. In this instruction his supreme courtesy to women again shone through.

5
CHRIST'S CONFIDENCE IN WOMEN

The woman at the well provides a good example, on two scores, of the confidence Christ displayed in women. The first needs no elaborating. It was his completely unembarrassed assumption that women would not misconstrue his approach to or friendship with them. Otherwise he would never have spoken to this woman in the first place. The second was his confidence in the *ability* of women, even such an unlikely one as she, to comprehend spiritual truth. Ryrie notes that some of Jesus' most profound revelations about himself and his Father were given in private teaching to women and concludes, "That He even did such a thing indicates His appreciation not only of the intellectual capacity in woman, but also their spiritual capabilities."

Let us look at his revelations to this "low, ignorant Samaritaness." To such a seemingly unlikely candidate for theological insights he offered "living water springing up into everlasting life." He told her the great fact that God is spirit, and that *where* he is worshiped is not the important point but *how,* "in spirit and in truth."

She was also the first person (as far as Scripture records) to whom he revealed that he was the Messiah. Why he chose this woman we are not told, but the effect was widespread. First she ran to the village and said to some of the men, "Come, see a man which told me all things that ever I did. Is not this the Christ?" Many of the Samaritans believed in Christ because of the woman's words: "So they besought him that he would tarry with them: and he abode there two days. And many more believed because of his own word" (Jn. 4:29, 40-42).

Martha and Mary To see another example of Christ's confidence in women we will look at that famous scene in the home of Martha, Mary and Lazarus (Lk. 10:38-42). This incident probably occurred during the Feast of Tabernacles, and, being near Jerusalem, this household may have been expecting a number of visitors. Possibly Martha had heard about the Master when the Seventy were sent out, as recorded by Luke at the beginning of chapter 10. At any rate, Martha "received him into her house," and possibly some of the disciples, too. So quite naturally she was very busy with "much serving," perhaps including footwashing as well as the preparation of food.

Mary, as the younger sister, had possibly done the foot-washing, but then had been captivated as the Lord began to speak to her about food for the soul. At any rate, she sat at his feet, listening, while Martha hurried back and forth and finally in exasperation came and said, "Lord, dost thou not care that my sister hath left me to serve alone? Bid her therefore that she help me."

Every woman who has ever been responsible for extensive hospitality can sympathize with Martha, and nearly every man, it seems, prefers to have a Martha around rather than a Mary. Yet what did Jesus say? With his usual courtesy and the gentlest of rebukes, he answered, "Martha, Martha, thou art careful and troubled about many things. But ... Mary hath chosen that good part, which shall not be taken away from her."

Recently I was given the witty little book *Are Women Human?* by Dorothy Sayers, well-known British scholar and novelist. In one essay she wryly states,

I think I have never heard a sermon preached on the story of Martha and Mary that did not attempt, somehow, somewhere, to explain away its text. Mary's, of course, was the better part—the Lord said so, and we must not precisely contradict Him. But we will be careful not to despise Martha. No doubt, he approved of her too. We could not get on without her, and indeed ... we greatly prefer her. For Martha was doing a really feminine job, whereas Mary was just behaving like any other disciple.

The Bible tells us Christ loved both Martha and Mary, however, and Martha's turn came for a great spiritual revelation. It was to her that Jesus spoke the astounding words which have brought comfort and hope to millions of people at Christian funerals: "I am the resurrection, and the life: he that believeth on me, though he were dead, yet shall he live: and whosoever liveth and believeth in me shall never die" (Jn. 11:25-26).

Easter Revelations Perhaps the most remarkable instance of Christ's confidence in women was when he gave the first revelation of his risen life to one or more women. As I read these Easter passages through in my first look at women in the Gospels, I wondered why Christ had given them this privilege of delivering the most startling piece of news the world has ever heard. Why not to Peter and John, the leading apostles, who apparently had been at that very spot just a few minutes before? I could only think that, being women, they would not be able to keep their mouths shut, whereas the men might keep it to themselves, thinking it too incredible to pass on without further evidence. Indeed, Christ later rebuked the eleven apostles "with their unbelief and hardness of heart, because they believed not them which had seen him after he was risen" (Mk. 16:14).

It was a surprise, therefore, to see Charles Ryrie's answer to this rather puzzling question:

The correct answer to the question of why God chose women to receive the news first has often been missed because it is so obvious. Women were honored with the news of the resurrection first simply because they were being faithful to womanly duties. . . . They were at the tomb . . . because they were bringing spices for the body. This was a woman's work. God so honored them because of their faithful performance of the responsibilities of their sex.

I had not heard of this womanly duty before, and Ryrie gives no source for his information. Certainly there is no indication of it in the Bible. Nicodemus and Joseph of Arimathea had already brought and applied nearly one hundred pounds of spices. John 19:40 tells us they wound the body in linen clothes "with the spices, as the manner of the Jews is to bury." In Acts 5:6 we are told that young men wound up the body of Ananias and buried it (without even waiting to inform the widow, apparently!).

Even if spicing dead bodies was a woman's duty, the reward seems out of all proportion to the duty. Why not give the privilege to Nicodemus and Joseph, who had already provided vast supplies of spices—and the tomb? Or to

John? He had had the courage to stay with Jesus during part of the trial and also to stand beside the cross, as well as to receive Mary into his home, something that could well have made his own mother jealous or made trouble with Mary's other children.

In any case, the women, like the apostles, seem to have completely ignored or forgotten Christ's teaching that he would be killed and rise the third day. If they had believed it, they would have realized there was no need for any spices. Actually, it was to the Twelve that the Lord had said he would rise again, and they may not even have told the women since it seems to have made so little impression on them. But even if the women had not heard from Christ or the disciples that he would rise again, they had heard the message of the angels (Lk. 24:4-6). Either they did not believe it or else the disciples talked them out of it, for the next time they went to the tomb the angel said to Mary, "Why weepest thou?" and she answered, "Because they have taken away my Lord, and I know not where they have laid him" (Jn. 20:13). Soon after that Christ revealed himself to Mary Magdalene.

Ryrie states that such instances as these "are ample proof of His revolutionary recognition of women, His confidence in their capabilities, and His concern for their education and welfare," but cautions us to remember that most of the Lord's teaching was given to men, and especially to the Twelve.

I do not want to give a disproportionate emphasis to woman's place in the Scriptures; certainly the greatest part of Christ's teaching was to the disciples and the crowds. Yet just as the promises of living water and resurrection are meant for all believers and not just the particular women addressed, may not the same be true of most of the teaching given first to men? Some have pointed out that the apostolic commission of John 20:19-23, Matthew 28:16-20 and Mark 16:15 was given to men only, but does this mean that only the eleven apostles were to "go into all the world and preach the gospel" or that only ten of them (since Thomas was not present when this authority was given) could pronounce forgiveness of sins? I have listened to sermons for over fifty years and have heard countless ministers preach on many of Christ's sayings to his disciples, but I have never heard even one minister warn the majority of his congregation that this was not for them. Are we supposed to keep reminding ourselves in the midst of a sermon that because we happen to have a uterus, a few extra curves and a more complicated nervous system, these words of Jesus cannot be for us?

Christ does not seem to have been concerned with such differences. When a woman in the crowd once called out how blessed were the womb and breasts which had formed and nourished him, he gave a surprising reply: "Yea rather, blessed are they that hear the word of God, and keep it" (Lk. 11:28). He implied that the physical properties of a woman, whether his own mother, or any other, are not the most important part of her. For the ideal disciple, man or woman, the important thing is hearing and obeying God's word. After all, only about one-third of the normal life span can be spent in child bearing, and if this is made the sole aim and purpose of woman's life the remaining years may prove empty and frustrating. Whatever our age, sex or circumstances, God still has a purpose for each life, and it is our privilege and responsibility to be attentive and obedient to his voice.

His Highest Praise   Finally, I would suggest that Christ showed his confidence in women by giving his highest praise to three of them. Others might, and in one case did, misconstrue their actions; Christ saw them for what they really were. To the Syrophoenician woman seeking healing for her daughter, he said, "Great is thy faith!" Others might have thought she was only concerned with getting her girl healed, exercising a selfish persistence at a source to which she was not entitled. Christ saw her action as the result of her understanding of who he was and of a real faith in his power and concern.

The disciples saw Mary's pouring of expensive ointment on Jesus' head as a sentimental extravagance. Christ recognized it as the result of her intuition motivated by her deep devotion and gratitude for what he had done in her life. And he promised that her act would be remembered and preached throughout the world as a memorial to her.

When he saw a poor widow put two mites into the offering box, he called his disciples over and said, "This poor widow hath cast more in, than all they which have cast into the treasury: for all they did cast in of their abundance; but she of her want did cast in all she had" (Mk. 12:43-44). Other people would not have regarded hers as a large offering and, if they had known it was all she had, would probably have called it foolish improvidence. Christ, however, gave her the credit for sacrificial giving of the highest order, and at the same time he established an entirely new criterion for giving: How much have we kept for ourselves?

So the Gospels give us proof that Christ regarded women as worth communicating with, as capable of comprehending deep spiritual truth, of exercising strong faith and of setting the highest standards of sacrificial giving.

6
WOMEN AT THE CROSS AND TOMB

The dread day of the crucifixion—the climax of God's great plan of salvation for all mankind—drew near. Surprisingly, the Gospels contain more references to women in connection with this event than with any other. Two of the women did not have direct contact with Jesus, but we mention them because the Holy Spirit has granted them a place in the inspired record.

The first was the maid in the palace of the high priest, where Christ was put on trial (Jn. 18:16-17). She appears to have been an observant girl who recognized Peter as having been in the company of the prisoner within. Here, perhaps, we might say God "used" this girl to bring about the fulfillment of Christ's prophecy that Peter would deny him three times that night and to reveal to Peter his own cowardice and weakness.

The other woman was Pilate's wife, who reinforced the verdict that Christ was righteous, not guilty. She obviously did not want her husband to condemn him, but rather (one hopes her protest indicated) wanted to see that he obtained justice. Pilate, however, out of a mistaken self-interest, took literally her words "have thou nothing to do with that just man," and publicly and ceremonially washed his hands of any responsibility in the matter (Mt. 27:11-26).

At the Cross Luke 23:27-29 tells us about the "great company of people and of women which bewailed and lamented" as Christ left the judgment hall carrying his cross through the streets toward Calvary. We do not know how many of these were real believers, but the rest of the women mentioned in the closing chapters of the Gospels were all "of his company" and remained faithful to the Lord in heart and presence throughout the long agony of the crucifixion.

While the Roman soldiers went through the hideous details of the crucifixion, passers-by railed on him; rulers, chief priests, scribes, elders and soldiers mocked him; but a group of women stood by the cross in the grip of grief and love. One of these was his mother, Mary. She was now experiencing, more excruciatingly than she could ever have dreamed, the prophecy of Simeon: "A sword shall pierce through thy own soul" (Lk. 2:35). Right there with her, unafraid of being personally identified with the one receiving a criminal's death sentence, was Mary's sister, Mary the wife of Cleophas, and Mary Magdalene (Jn. 19:25).

In addition, standing by the cross was also "the disciple whom Jesus loved," whom we assume was John. The Lord, in the midst of his own fierce agony, had loving thought and compassion for his mother and put her in John's keeping with the words, "Woman, behold thy son!" and to John, "Behold thy mother!" "From that hour that disciple took her unto his own home" (Jn. 19:26-27). This may seem a strange arrangement to us since we know that Jesus had half-brothers and half-sisters who presumably could have taken care of Mary and also that John had his own mother, who was right there at the scene (Mt. 27:56). Perhaps the main purpose, as in his two former remarks to his mother, was once again to leave no ground for the deification of Mary. The fact that he addressed her as "Woman" yet referred to her as John's "mother" seems to indicate that she was no longer to be regarded as having any unique relationship to him.

As the various phenomena accompanying the sacrificial death of the Son of God took place—the darkness, the earthquake, the rending of the temple veil and the amazing way Christ deliberately ended his life after three hours (instead of the crucifixion's dragging on for several days as was usually the case)—the centurion in charge of the executions exclaimed, "Truly this was the Son of God" (Mt. 27:54). The multitude who had merely come to watch the spectacle returned to the city "smiting their breasts." But, as Matthew, Mark and Luke all tell us, many women remained, beholding from afar the tortured bodies on the crosses. Among these were Mary Magdalene, Mary the mother of James and Joses, Salome and many others who "followed Jesus from Galilee, ministering unto him" (Mt. 27:55). Mark, besides listing the same names adds, "and many other women which came up with him to Jerusalem" (Mk. 15:41). These had all traveled nearly a hundred miles and were in the city to celebrate the Passover. Possibly they had hoped to see Jesus claim the throne of Israel. They had hardly come that distance just to bring spices for his dead body.

When Joseph of Arimathea and Nicodemus took the body of Jesus to a new tomb in a nearby garden, Mary Magdalene, Mary the mother of Joses, and other women from Galilee took note of where he was buried and made plans to return with additional spices as soon as the Sabbath passed (Mk. 15:47; Lk. 23:55-56).

That Terrifying Easter Morning At very early dawn after the Sabbath, the two Marys, Joanna and possibly some other women, went to the garden, wondering as they hurried along whom they could get to help them roll away the huge stone from the entrance to the tomb. Evidently none of the apostles had thought of going, at least so early.

As these women drew near to the garden, there was an earthquake, and an angel of the Lord rolled away the stone, terrifying the guards (Mt. 28:2-4). The women looked in and saw that the body of Jesus was not there. Then two dazzling angels appeared and spoke to them: "Why seek ye the living among the dead? He is not here, but is risen." The women fled, trembling, and "told all these things unto the eleven, and to all the rest" (Lk. 24:5-9). Unfortunately, to the apostles the women's words "seemed as idle tales, and they believed them not." However, Peter and John did take the trouble to go to the tomb to have a look and saw that the Master's body was no longer there.

Mary Magdalene apparently followed them back to the garden, and, though they returned after looking in the tomb, she, in her desperate grief and her uncertainty about what the angels had really meant, stood outside the opening, weeping. Finally she looked in and saw angels at the head and foot of the hewn-out shelf where the body of Christ had lain. They asked her why she wept, and she replied, "Because they have taken away my Lord, and I know not where they have laid him" (Jn. 21:13). She was still evidently thinking of Jesus as a dead body.

She turned outside again and saw Jesus without recognizing him until, in his own inimitable, compassionate way he said her name, "Mary." Then she flung herself at his feet, and he commissioned her to "Go tell my brethren that they go into Galilee" (Mt. 28:10).

In addition to the reason I suggested in chapter 4, perhaps Christ first showed himself to women rather than men because these women showed personal devotion to the Master himself while the male disciples were preoccupied with thoughts of his kingdom and the positions they would have in it. When, unrecognized, he joined the two discouraged disciples returning to Emmaus, Cleopas told about the crucifixion and added, "But we trusted that it had been he which should have redeemed Israel" (Lk. 24:21), presumably meaning from the power of Rome. Even when the disciples gathered to meet him immediately before the ascension, they still asked, "Lord, wilt thou at this time restore again the kingdom to Israel?" (Acts 1:6). The women, with the possible exception of the mother of James and John, seem more drawn to the Person of Christ than to his kingdom.

Some men may suggest that women's attraction to Christ is due to the unconscious sex appeal of a male figure. It is conceivable that one reason most churches have had a majority of women worshipers, especially in earlier days when extremely few were involved in the business world, is that some women welcomed personal contact with a male figure in the form of the minister. I cannot believe, however, that women are likely to have a similar feeling about the Person of Christ. Women are drawn to him because he understands them perfectly, loves them as individual persons and has demonstrated this love by giving his perfect life for their sins. Search as we may in the Gospels, we never find him belittling or degrading women, but quite the reverse.

Dorothy Sayers describes the situation in a delightful way:

Perhaps it was no wonder the women were . . . last at the cross. They had never known a man like this Man—there never has been such another. A prophet and teacher who never nagged at them, never flattered or coaxed or patronized; who never made sick jokes about them. . . . who rebuked without querulousness and praised without condescension; who took their questions and arguments seriously; who never mapped out their sphere for them, never urged them to be feminine or jeered at them for being female; who had no axe to grind and no uneasy male dignity to defend; who took them as he found them and was completely unself-conscious. There is no act, no sermon, no parable in the whole Gospel that borrows its pungency from female perversity; nobody could possibly guess from the words and deeds of Jesus that there was anything "funny" [or, we might add, "inferior"] about woman's nature.

There is no doubt that men and women cannot understand each other perfectly and completely, just because each has some difference in physical structure and function which the other cannot experience. Christ is the only one who can fully understand both sexes, because he created them: In the image of God, "male and female created he them" (Gen. 1:27). Therefore, as Dorothy Sayers points out, in spite of Christ's example of treating women as ordinary human beings, "his Church to this day" does not quite seem to share his view. The reason its spokesmen would probably give for this, of course, is that the scriptural revelation is not limited to the Gospels. So we must examine the remaining books of the New Testament to find out what took place in the early churches and what the Holy Spirit has added to the inspired text on the subject of woman.

At this point we can only conclude from our study of the Gospels that they contain no confirmation that the wealthy matron of Proverbs was necessarily God's "ideal woman," only that Christ had great concern, compassion and commendation for women in many different circumstances. He also committed to some of them new spiritual revelations and responsibilities. The one condition found for pleasing God was hearing and doing his will, and there is no record in the Gospels that his will for woman was in any way different from his will for any other of his followers.

II

WOMAN IN ACTS

7
WOMEN IN THE FIRST CHURCHES

Luke's account of the formation of the early church, recorded in the book of Acts, is certainly one of the most thrilling parts of the Bible. In addition to its general interest and inspiration, it also has some exciting insights about women. I noted thirty-three references to women in Acts, and although this is comparatively few for the size of the book, it is highly significant in comparison with the history of most world religions. These references also indicate a wide range of activity for women within the early church.

Five verses merely refer to famous female figures inconsequential to our study: Pharaoh's daughter, credited by Stephen with saving the life of the baby Moses (7:21); Candace, in whose royal service was the eunuch converted through Philip's witness in the desert (8:27); Drusilla, wife of the governor Felix (24:24); and Bernice, sister of King

Agrippa (25:23), both of whom joined the men out of curiosity about the new religion Paul proclaimed when he made his defense; and lastly, the many-breasted goddess Diana, worshiped as mother of gods and men, whose temple at Ephesus was one of the Seven Wonders of the World and whose worship was threatened by Paul's preaching.

A sixth tantalizing reference mentions a woman famous by association only—Paul's sister (23:16). From it we can only glean that she had a brave and resourceful son evidently in sympathy with his uncle Paul.

The remaining incidents involving women we will consider under eight headings denoting the significance of women's place in and contribution to the early Christian church.

Full Members *They were full members.* In almost every place where the gospel was preached, women, both Jew and Greek, are mentioned as being among those who believed.

In Jerusalem, "multitudes both of men and women" believed (5:14). We are also told that the disciples "daily in the temple, and in every house, ceased not to teach and preach Jesus Christ" (5:42). This house-preaching would certainly have involved the women very directly in housecleaning and hospitality, and presumably they were fully integrated in the homes and not confined to a separate section as in the synagogues.

Further afield, in Samaria both men and women believed as a result of Philip's preaching (8:12), while at Joppa were Dorcas and many other women (9:36-43). At Lystra lived Timothy's mother Eunice (16:1), a Jewess whom we know was a believer, as was her own mother Lois (2 Tim. 1:5).

At Philippi Lydia, the first Christian convert in Europe, was a charter member of one of the most encouraging churches founded by Paul; and there were other women there also (16:13-15). In Thessalonica there believed and associated with Paul "of the devout Greeks a great multitude, and of the chief women not a few" (17:4). In Berea many believed: "of honourable women which were Greeks, and of men, not a few" (17:12).

The greatest number of women believers mentioned were in Macedonia, but even in Athens, where the response to Paul's preaching was small, a man named Dionysius, important because he was a member of the Areopagus, believed, and also "a woman named Damaris, and others" (17:34).

We are not told why some of these women are described as "honourable." Most commentators assert that it refers to their social status, which seems to give an unpleasant touch of snobbishness to the early church, but we can hope that the term applied equally well to their character as they developed in the Christian life. Certainly Priscilla, a refugee from Rome, played an important part in the founding and establishing of the churches at Corinth and Ephesus; and Paul's later comment that she, together with her husband, "were ready to lay down their necks" for his and the gospel's sake (Rom. 16:4), points to her character rather than her social status.

These women were not merely listeners and believers in the gospel; they were baptized into full membership. Under the Old Testament order only men could partake of circumcision, the outward sign that they were God's people. Some of the Jewish believers from Judea had actually gone and told the new Christians at Antioch, "Except ye be circumcised after the manner of Moses, ye cannot be saved" (15:11), showing how vital a part of Jewish thinking it was. But Acts clearly indicates women's equal place as members of the body of Christ: "When they believed . . . they were baptized, both men and women" (8:12). Lydia was baptized and her household, and also the Philippian jailor "and all his" (16:15, 33).

Thus women who only recently had been recognized as and included in Christ's company, now were able to enjoy full membership in his body, the church. This must have been a wonderful liberation from the thinking of Judaism as expressed in the view of one first-century rabbi, Eliazer, who stated, "Rather should the words of the Torah be burned than entrusted to a woman. Whoever teaches his daughter the Torah is like one who teaches her lasciviousness."

Participants in Prayer Meetings *They joined in prayer meetings.* We are told of this in at least three various locations and circumstances.

The first was immediately after Christ's ascension into heaven, when the one hundred and twenty or so disciples were waiting for the coming of the Holy Spirit whom Christ had promised. We are told that the eleven apostles "continued with one accord in prayer and supplication with the women, and Mary the mother of Jesus, and with his brethren" (1:14).

The second was connected with Peter's imprisonment by Herod after Herod saw that his execution of James pleased the Jewish leaders. The believers were fervently praying in the home of Mary, mother of John Mark, that a similar fate would not soon take Peter from them. We are even given the name of one of the other women there, Rhoda, who went to the door in response to Peter's knocking, after an angel had miraculously freed him from prison in the middle of the night. Rhoda was so overcome with joy at hearing

Peter's voice that she forgot to open the door and ran back to interrupt the praying with the announcement that Peter was outside. The others could not believe the swift answer to their prayers and rather rudely told her, "Thou art mad!" Peter had to keep up a continual, but probably muted, tattoo before they would finally open the door.

Finally, we move to Europe, and the city of Philippi. In spite of its being an important trading center and Roman garrison, there were evidently not enough Jewish men to rate a synagogue (ten was the minimum) and the few worshipers of Jehovah, in this case all women, met each Sabbath at the riverside to pray. Luke tells us, "And on the sabbath we went out of the city by a river side, where prayer was wont to be made, and we sat down, and spake unto the women which resorted there" (16:13). It was well that on this occasion Paul ignored the custom which dictated that a "good" man, and especially a rabbi, should not address a woman in public, for it was as a result of his speaking that Lydia believed, and one of the healthiest New Testament churches was formed in her home. Perhaps it was in response to the earnest prayers of these women that God sent Paul to them.

Spirit-filled Prophets *They were filled with the Spirit and prophesied.* On the day of Pentecost, Luke tells us, "they were all with one accord in one place" (2:1). Presumably these "all" were the same people mentioned in 1:14-15. If so, then the fiery tongues came on the women also.

Luke goes on to say, "They were all filled with the Holy Spirit, and began to speak with other tongues, as the Spirit gave them utterance" (2:4). Some commentators assume that only the Twelve were filled and spoke, but the Greek does not specify males, contrary to the AV's translation of

77

the words uttered by the amazed bystanders: "These *men* are full of new wine" (2:13).

Peter explained the phenomenon taking place this way: "These are not drunken . . . but this is that which was spoken by the prophet Joel; . . . I will pour out of my Spirit on *all* flesh: and your sons and your daughters shall prophesy, . . . and on my servants and on my handmaidens I will pour out in those days of my Spirit, and they shall prophesy" (2:15-18). Thus, it seems probable that Peter was indicating that the women, too, were manifesting the evidences of the Spirit's having come upon them, and were telling the "wonderful works of God."

Strangely enough, I had never noticed the female element in Joel's prophecy before, and it seems to have escaped the notice of all the commentators as well. Yet surely this prophecy constitutes strong ground for the justification of a spiritual ministry in some form for women. The clear repetition, sons and *daughters,* servants and *handmaids,* seems to leave no doubt of God's intention to include, right from the beginning of the new church age, both male and female among his prophetic or teaching servants. Not only that, but this would seem to be a glorious proclamation that in the new spiritual order just as all are equally saved by Christ's blood so the Spirit will be poured upon them irrespective of seniority, sex or social status; and all will be empowered to minister with his help.

On turning to Joel 2:15-29, I was interested to note, too, that Joel had called the people together in a solemn assembly—men, women (including new brides and nursing mothers) and children—that they might all hear and enjoy the promise of the good things to come.

Finally, in Acts 21:9, some other women who fulfilled Joel's prophecy are mentioned: "And the same man [Philip] had four daughters, virgins, which did prophesy."

Establishers and Supporters of Local Churches *They helped establish and support local churches.* The first convert from Paul's preaching in Europe, as already mentioned, was a woman named Lydia. Lydia was apparently a successful businesswoman "whose heart the Lord opened," as Luke beautifully expresses it. She was already a worshiper of God, doing her best to obey him by meeting on the Sabbath for prayer with a few other women.

Since she refers to "my house" and Luke refers to "her household," we assume she was single or, more probably, a widow with a considerable domestic and business staff. On believing the gospel she and her household were immediately baptized, and then with considerable insistence invited Paul and his party to stay in her home. The doubtful propriety with which some in other cultures might view this cannot have been a factor to be considered, probably because of the numerous persons already in her household. However, one commentator, at least, feels Paul must have married Lydia! She was very forthright in her appeal based on whether he judged her "faithful to the Lord"—and evidently she passed the test with Paul.

More believers, including men, were added to their number, and they apparently met at Lydia's house, for after Paul's painful beating and imprisonment for a night and the request of the magistrates that he move on, he went straight to Lydia's house, had a last farewell with "the brethren" and then departed (16:40).

In Athens, as we also saw earlier, one man and one woman, Damaris, were leaders among the believers Paul left after his short visit. In Thessalonica, Berea, Damascus, Joppa, Samaria and Jerusalem, women were also disciples and charter members of the churches there.

Corinth is of particular interest because there Priscilla not only shared in her husband Aquila's business but also had an important place in the church. Paul not only lived in their home for eighteen months but also worked beside them at the same trade, and therefore had ample opportunity to evaluate her life and character. Later he wrote to the Romans, "Greet Priscilla and Aquila my helpers in Christ Jesus: who have for my life laid down their own necks: unto whom not only I give thanks, but also *all the churches of the Gentiles*" (Rom. 16:3-4). Possibly Priscilla had no children and therefore had more time for Christian work. Also, she was probably cosmopolitan in outlook, able to understand the cultural backgrounds of the various believers, since she and her husband had been living and working in Italy until Claudius ordered all Jews to leave Rome.

When Paul finally left Corinth, Priscilla and Aquila accompanied him on the ship to Ephesus and, while Paul went on to Jerusalem, settled there, in yet another new city and country, to undertake the dangerous work of establishing another church in their home. It was while they were at Ephesus that Apollos, the Alexandrian, visited there, eloquently preaching "the way of the Lord [but] knowing only the baptism of John." Priscilla and her husband, having tasted the joy of knowing Christ personally, were anxious that Apollos should have this experience, too, and recognized how much his gift of eloquence and boldness could be used to bring others to Christ. Accordingly, although this man was "mighty in the scriptures" (18:24), Priscilla and Aquila did not let awe or false modesty keep them from trying to minister to him. They invited him to their home "and expounded unto him the way of God more perfectly." Apollos' true greatness is revealed in his gratefully receiving instruction from this lay man and woman team, and he put it to good use, later turning many others to Christ through his preaching (18:24-28).

Victims of Persecution *They were persecuted for their faith.* No doubt it was because women were so integral a part of and such real assistance to the early church that young Saul of Tarsus had no compunction about dragging them away from home and children to prison and hopefully to death. Luke tells us of Paul's zeal in entering "every house" in Jerusalem, looking for those he regarded as heretics, and even in planning to go to Damascus to drag them bound to Jerusalem for trial (8:3 and 9:2). Paul himself admitted later, "I persecuted this way unto the death, binding and delivering into prisons both men and women" (22:4).

In Antioch of Pisidia, some Jewish women served as persecutors rather than as the ones being persecuted. This incident contains a real touch of irony. After Paul had preached Christ in the synagogue, "the Jews stirred up the devout and honourable women, and the chief men of the city, and raised persecution against Paul and Barnabas." Since the Jews did not allow women in the inner temple court nor permit them in the main area of the synagogue nor even count them in the quorum of persons needed for worship, this act of making them the forefront of opposition against the Christians seems to me a little inconsistent and despicable!

Doers of Charity *They engaged in charitable work.* It is no surprise to find a woman doing acts of charity in the early church. Rather, it is remarkable that only one occurrence of this is mentioned (especially when we consider how many

tens of thousands of women have labored dutifully to produce every variety of wearable and unwearable garment
for some Dorcas Society).

Tabitha (or Dorcas) certainly is an example par excel-
lence of practical Christian love, and, interestingly, she is
the only woman in the New Testament actually called *disciple*. It seems probable that she helped all in need, not just
fellow believers, for when Peter came to her deathbed "all
the widows stood by weeping" and showed him the clothes
Dorcas had made for them (9:39). After turning them out
of the room Peter raised Dorcas from death and "called the
saints and widows" (9:41). I find no justification elsewhere
in the Bible for assuming that a widow cannot be a saint, so
it appears that he called the believers and the other widows
Dorcas had helped.

Although the incident is not exactly in the same category,
here would be as convenient a place as any to include the
reference in Acts 21 to the women who expressed sorrow
and sympathy as they accompanied husbands and children
in escorting Paul from Tyre to where he was to embark on
the dangerous journey to Jerusalem. They all had a fore-
boding that this would lead to his death and so did all they
could to show their love and concern.

Acts mentions one area of practical service which we
might think would naturally fall to women, namely, that of
"serving tables." Yet surprisingly this was allocated to men,
and men with high spiritual qualifications at that. In Acts 6
we read that in the very early days after Pentecost, when the
believers were living in a close communal fellowship, there
was a "daily ministration." After a while the Grecian Jewish
converts complained that their widows were being neglected by the local Hebrews. Was this an imaginary slight, or
was it an oversight by the busy apostles to whom those who

sold land gave the proceeds for the communal need? We are not told. We only know that the twelve apostles decided they should not let anything interfere with their primary work of preaching and prayer. Instead, they told the believers to choose out seven *men*, full of faith and the Holy Spirit, for this work of "serving tables."

It was the expression "serving tables," together with "daily ministration," which had made me formerly think of the incident in terms of food, just as J. B. Phillips translates it, "in the daily distribution of food." I learned recently, however, that in the Coverdale Bible of 1535 the phrase is rendered as the "daylie handreachinge," and F. F. Bruce assumes it to be the distribution of money from the communal fund. This would certainly make it easier to detect differences of allocations between Hebrew and Greek widows and would better explain why *men* were appointed for the work. In any case, the fact that they were to be full of faith and the Holy Spirit is a reminder that *all* that we do for the Lord is holy, needing our dedicated attention, whether it is serving soup, balancing accounts or whatever.

Recipients of God's Healing Power *They were the recipients of miraculous healings.* Although there is no doubt that she was among the most deserving of all those the Bible records as having been raised from the dead, the mention of Dorcas' charitable acts was perhaps merely incidental to the miracle Peter performed in restoring her to life.

A very different case of the healing of a woman was Paul's healing of a demon-possessed slave girl at Philippi, who had the gift of clairvoyance and could tell fortunes with apparent accuracy. Paul appears very human here, and probably many of us could identify with him in the motive which prompted him to heal her! Instead of being full of compassion for this girl in her sad condition, as we can imagine Christ would have been, Paul was irritated by the nuisance of her constant following and calling out after his party as they went to the place of prayer by the river. Although the AV says "grieved," which could be taken in another sense, the original meaning is rather "vexed," or, as J. B. Phillips puts it, "She continued this behavior for many days, and then Paul, in a burst of irritation, turned round and spoke to the spirit in her, 'I command you in the name of Jesus Christ to come out of her!' " (16:18). The girl was instantly delivered, and lost the power of fortunetelling.

Perhaps Paul had been aware that driving the evil spirit out of her would mean trouble from her masters, both for the slave girl and himself, as indeed proved to be the case when he and Silas were cruelly beaten and thrown into prison. This, however, led to the remarkable conversion of the jailor and all his house. We do not know what happened to the slave girl, but, since she already had the insight that Paul and Silas were messengers from the most high God and were able to tell the way of salvation, we may hope that she truly believed and that her sister in the faith, Lydia, was able to buy her from her masters, since she was no longer of any particular value to them. If not, her fate does not bear thinking about in the face of her masters' anger and their frustration at the loss of such an easy and considerable income.

Responsible Sinners *They were held accountable for sin.* The only remaining reference to a woman is a sad and frightening one: that of Ananias and his wife, Sapphira (5:1-11). One might have imagined that it was the wife's deceitful scheme to save a little money, but the Bible tells us clearly that it was merely "with her full knowledge" that Ananias planned and practiced the deception.

Here we have the Adam and Eve situation reversed. Paul laid the greater blame for their original sin on Eve (1 Tim. 2:14), but Peter indicated plainly that it was Satan who put this scheme in the husband's heart and blamed Sapphira merely because she "agreed" to the plan—and that in spite of the fact that later, in his first letter, he would tell wives they should be in subjection to their husbands.

But God held her equally culpable because she had evidently not condemned the sin of her husband and had prepared to tell a lie to support his falsehood. Therefore, when it comes to a moral issue, a woman cannot be blindly obedient to a husband and shelter under the "weaker sex" label. We must face the solemn fact that since woman has been given a significant place, and equal membership, in the body of those redeemed by Christ's blood, she must also recognize that God requires the same high moral standard from every disciple, man or woman, since there is in his sight neither male nor female.

Can we find God's ideal woman in the book of the Acts? Was it Lydia, successful businesswoman and a charter member of the church at Philippi, a woman whose heart the Lord opened? Or equally capable and hardworking Priscilla, able to teach the great biblical scholar Apollos more fully about Christ? Or Dorcas, constantly busy with her needle for the poor widows? (She would certainly seem to be the choice of most commentators!) Or Mary, John Mark's mother, who hospitably opened her home? We are given no clue about which of the women in Acts is God's ideal. But we can be reasonably sure it was not Sapphira.

III

WOMAN IN THE EPISTLES

8
WOMAN IN GENERAL: CHILDBEARING AND ADORNMENT

This section proved a much less pleasant, and much more difficult, study than that in the Gospels and Acts. In the former we found Christ's amazing tenderness, courtesy and interest in women and their spiritual growth while in Acts we saw the exciting historical account of the conversion of various women and their active place in the early church. In the Epistles, however, we find a few restrictive instructions for female believers, suggestive of an inferior status, and we see that Paul occasionally has some unpleasant things to say about woman in general; for example, that it was the first *woman* who was deceived by the devil. In the letter to the Romans he mentions female as well as male sexual perverts while in the ones to Timothy he speaks of "silly women laden with sins" and "old wives' fables." This sounds rather different from any of Christ's words about women. Paul does, however, send warm and appreciative greetings to individual women whose help in the gospel he has experienced, and he also makes some revolutionary statements about the marriage relationship.

There are two main difficulties in studying woman in the Epistles. The first is determining what exactly the writers said, and intended, in the original languages. Since some of the AV renderings have given rise to some of the confusions, I had hoped at first to ascertain this from the various English translations of the Bible, but this proved impossible. We have it on the highest authority that there are in Paul's letters "some things hard to be understood" (2 Pet. 3:16). Part of the difficulty arises from the concepts dealt with, but part also from the language. Donald Guthrie in *New Testament Introduction* tells us that Paul "inclines away from literary Greek towards the vernacular, yet is not a good example of that. He is too individualistic, too given to frequent diversions of thought, too often apt to express himself in broken syntax. In a sense, the style is as adaptable as the man." I certainly can make no claim to an exhaustive study since I know little Greek and since this book was researched amid a busy yet often circumscribed life as a missionary wife and mother with traveling, speaking engagements and various odd jobs and residence in four countries. However, I think I have been able to indicate most of the main views on the subjects dealt with in this section.

The second difficulty arises from the very nature of letters. While we have no problem deciding that the message of David's letter to Joab—"Set ye Uriah in the forefront of the hottest battle . . . that he may be smitten, and die" (2 Sam. 11:15)—was limited to one occasion, when we read Paul's letters of instruction to Timothy the issue is not quite so clear. For example, Paul says, "Drink no longer water, but use a little wine for thy stomach's sake and thine often infirmities" (1 Tim. 5:23). Is this command for everyone with a stomach ailment or infirmity? Some people regard *1 Tim., 2 Cor.* and so on merely as convenient tags for finding verses, giving no thought for the persons to whom the letters were addressed. They regard every instruction of Paul as binding on the church today, using the same logic as well-meaning persons who affirm these lines: "Every promise in the Book is mine; Every chapter, every verse, every line." But surely some thought must be given to context.

While in Christ there is neither male nor female, as he himself often demonstrated and as Paul explicitly states in Galatians 3:28, the fact remains that God did create two complementary biological sexes; thus it was natural for the new churches, established in the midst of a completely heathen environment, to seek guidance on marital, social and spiritual spheres from their missionary, Paul. But whether every detail of his answers applies to all Christians of all times is not always easy to determine; or whether, when he speaks about woman, he is referring to all women or merely to wives, since every woman in those days was expected to marry young. (A girl was considered to be of age at twelve-and-a-half years.)

One might think that the more detailed instructions about woman in the Epistles would make it possible to discern "God's ideal woman" there. Yet in them she sometimes appears rather different from God's supposed ideal in Proverbs 31. These variations could be due to differences between an agrarian and an urban culture and the desired qualities of a wife in each. But this again points to the probability that God does not have a final blueprint of the ideal woman. Further, since in addition to generalizations about woman in the Epistles there are also instructions to specific groups (older and younger women, virgins, wives, widows), it seems legitimate to assume that "the exemplary Christian matron," favored by many commentators, is not necessarily God's ideal. Nor is it invariably true, as one states, that a woman "only in connection with her husband attains her proper dignity and worth." These qualities may be found in a single person, too, and in one place Paul advocates the unmarried state for both males and females.

Since the references to woman in the Epistles are made by different writers, and for varying purposes, we will study them under the specific categories mentioned above. But first we will consider some aspects of woman in general. As I studied the verses dealing with woman I began to realize that one rarely hears most of them preached on. It is curious that some pronouncements about woman are almost completely disregarded by Christians today while a few are treated as having great weight. Finally I saw a pattern: Things said just about woman usually are not interesting or do not seem important to male theologians. Instructions dealing with her relationship to man, on the other hand, are regarded with the utmost gravity.

Childbearing I am considering the childbearing function of woman first for two reasons. It is the most obvious and unique physical ability of woman and the main purpose for which many people consider her to have been created. Also it leads to a good illustration of the difficulty in understanding some of the verses about woman.

The verse in question here is 1 Timothy 2:15: "Notwithstanding she [the woman] shall be saved in childbearing, if they continue in faith and charity and holiness with sobriety." I was hesitant to consider this in isolation from its context, but there is so much uncertainty about this verse that many commentators deal with it in that way (or not at all) since, curiously, it comes at the end of a section often headed "Instructions for Worship." Also some of the points mentioned in that paragraph are the subjects of later chapters in this book. Suffice it to say here that Paul begins by urging men to pray everywhere with uplifted hands, then speaks on women's dress and status (in the church?). He does not allow the woman to teach or be dictatorial to the man: "For Adam was first formed, then Eve. And Adam was not beguiled, but the woman being beguiled hath fallen into transgression: but she shall be saved through her [or the] childbearing, if they continue in faith and love and sanctification with sobriety" (1 Tim. 2:12-15, ASV).

The problems in verse 15 are obvious, and Bible translators have been rather free in manipulating it to make it say something that sounds sensible to them. One of the simplest techniques is changing the plural into the singular. Instead of *they* we have in the RSV "Woman will be saved through bearing children, if *she* continue . . ." with a footnote to say the Greek is plural. The New International Version (NIV), the latest translation by conservative scholars, has both in the plural: "Women will be kept safe [footnote: 'be saved'] through childbirth, if they continue in faith. . . ." The NEB has "Yet she will be saved through motherhood [footnote: '*Or* saved through the Birth of the Child, *or* brought safely through childbirth']—if only women continue in faith . . ." and a footnote alternative, "if only husband and wife continue in mutual fidelity."

These quotations indicate the major problem of this verse. What is the "saving" that is promised, conditionally, to women? Is it spiritual salvation, which they can only earn through bearing children and having, in addition to faith, love, holiness and propriety? Or is it a promise of safe delivery during childbirth provided she, or she and her husband, have faith, love, holiness and sobriety?

Modern theologians and translators tend to think this verse refers to the dangers of childbirth since the first view creates an obvious theological problem. J. B. Phillips' paraphrase has "I believe that women will come safely through childbirth if they maintain a life of faith, love and gravity."

The trouble with this theory is that it does not appear to accord with the facts of life. Those of us who have lived in more primitive (and usually non-Christian) societies have observed that tribal women often have easier deliveries than their more "civilized" (and sometimes Christian) sisters. A missionary doctor friend of mine has suggested that the oriental practice of squatting for some forms of work, for resting and for elimination purposes may also make for easier delivery.

Again, while waiting to sail for China I spent three months helping in a Christian home established for unmarried expectant mothers. During that time, although most of the twenty-five girls certainly did not meet Paul's specifications, all except one had uncomplicated deliveries, easily handled by midwives.

Conversely, most of us have known some godly Christian women who have experienced great difficulty, and even death, in childbirth. In the Bible, Rachel died in childbirth right after Jacob had built the altar at Bethel and the whole family had cleansed themselves and thrown away their idols, Rachel having harbored her father's family images for twenty years. Surely at this time she was most likely to be pleasing to God.

Some men are sure the word *saved* must be taken in a spiritual sense and that Paul must be referring to the birth of Christ since he is the true means of salvation. As we have noted, the NEB gives as an alternative reading "saved through the Birth of the Child." Donald Guthrie, however, in *The Pastoral Epistles* says the passage cannot refer to the birth of the Messiah because the Greek article is generic, referring to the whole process of childbearing rather than to one particular instance.

Walter Lock, in the *International Critical and Exegetical Commentary*, believes that Paul means "they shall be spiritually saved" not merely physically preserved because Paul is still thinking of the idea expressed in verse 4 that God "will have all men to be saved and to come unto the knowledge of the truth." A stronger ground for this meaning could be the paragraph which ends with this verse on childbearing. Paul's quick mind jumps ahead, not always spelling out the logical steps. He has said he does not let women teach, or dominate, "the man" since Adam was formed first, then Eve, and "Adam was not the one deceived; it was the woman who was deceived and became a sinner" (NIV). Does Paul then remember God's words to Eve about bearing children, and intend a note of encouragement that Timothy may pass on to the church women: Just be good, and all will go well? Or is there an ominous hint that woman is the specially wicked half of humanity and must perpetually pay for her sin with painful childbirths? We shall consider this view in depth later. For now it is enough to state that this opinion has been held, and is implied in the very complicated paraphrase of the Amplified New Testament: "Nevertheless (the sentence put upon women [of pain in motherhood] does not hinder their [souls'] salvation) and they will be saved [eternally] if they continue in faith and love and holiness, with self-control; [saved indeed] through the Child-bearing, that is, by the birth of the [divine] Child."

So strong has been this idea that at first many people, especially ministers, were highly critical of the use of analgesics for women during childbirth on the ground that it would nullify God's "curse" on them and perhaps even endanger their salvation. The latter threat must have been especially important since the former argument seems never to have been advanced against power mowers, tractors and other labor-saving devices calculated to reduce considerably the sweat on men's brows, and thus the "curse" put upon them!

Whatever view one takes of the difficult first part of the verse, the problem remains: This "saving" appears to be dependent on some mature Christian virtues in the woman; and I have found no one who tries to explain this. A typical modern commentary on the passage is that of Paul F. Barackman:

2:13-15 One of the difficult passages in these letters. But we may note these facts. First, Paul's concern was mainly with married couples at this point. Secondly, for Paul the Scripture . . . supported his argument by the priority of Adam's creation, and the initiative of Eve in the first sin. Thirdly, generally speaking, verse 15 may be taken to mean that woman's honor is found in her intended sphere, taking her place in the home and exemplifying Christian virtues.

This certainly leaves some things unexplained, including why only mothers are to experience the "curse" on women.

Another highly regarded modern theologian, William Hendriksen, boldly assures us:

The complete thought is as follows: if the women members of the church will abide in faith, love and sanctification, meanwhile exercising proper self-control and reserve, they will find their joy and salvation in bearing children to God's glory, yes, in all the duties and delights of Christian motherhood.

This still leaves us with a problem. Where did Martha and Mary, and probably Mary Magdalene, plus countless single and childless women since them find their joy and salvation? It seems to me that the commentators who maintain that no one really knows what this verse means are nearest the truth.

One other possible explanation has occurred to me since reading A. Cohen's *Everyman's Talmud*. In it he tells us that the rabbinic teaching of the Pharisees was that Satan performs three functions: He seduces people; he accuses them before God; he inflicts the punishment of death. He particularly accuses people before God "only in times of danger." Thus, "At the time of childbirth the angel of death (i.e. Satan) becomes the accuser of the mother" (Eccles. R. III 2.). Another teaching was that certain classes of persons are particularly susceptible to attack by evil spirits and need special protection: an invalid, a woman in confinement, a bridegroom and a bride.

Since Paul had studied under Rabbi Gamaliel of the Hillel school, whose teaching, according to Edersheim, "placed tremendous emphasis upon Jewish oral traditions," and since Paul himself was, as he tells us, a Pharisee "taught according to the perfect manner of the law of the fathers" (Acts 22:3), these teachings would have been well-known to him. Thus when he mentioned Eve's being deceived by Satan his mind may have jumped to Satan's accusing women before God at childbirth. In this way he could legitimately suggest that if a woman had faith, love and holiness she would have nothing to fear when Satan accused her before God. This seems more logical than the idea that a woman must live a mature Christian life if she is either to be saved spiritually or to come safely through childbirth.

All we can be absolutely sure of, however, is that childbearing is a function of women and that faith, love, holiness and self-control are very important characteristics for her, as for every believer.

In contrast to the complexities of 1 Timothy 2:15 another reference to childbirth is Paul's sublimely simple statement, "God sent forth his Son, made of a woman . . . that we might receive the adoption of sons" (Gal. 4:4-5). What an incredible honor for humanity's supposed second-class sex! God could so easily have created a second Adam in baby form, to be legally adopted into a Davidic family. Some early Moslems even believed that God would miraculously cause a special baby to be born from a male, and that is why their men traditionally wore baggy pants tied at the ankle —to catch the baby when it suddenly and miraculously arrived. But in fact it was to a humble woman's body that God chose to entrust his sinless Son.

Through a woman sin first came into the world, but God in his love and mercy planned that through a woman also should come the Redeemer for the sin of the whole world. Through faith in this woman's perfectly human yet perfectly sinless seed all may be adopted as children into God's family. We can assume that the particular girl chosen for this honor must have been close to God's ideal, but as we saw in our study of the Gospels there are few details about the young Mary, except her thoughtfulness, knowledge of the Scripture and a complete willingness for God's will.

The Epistles contain a few other references to childbearing, under the topic of widows remarrying.

Adornment, Dress and Disposition   Next to her ability to bear children, probably the most obvious topic associated with woman is dress and adornment. And both Peter and

Paul express views on this subject. In 1 Timothy 2:9 Paul states that women should adorn themselves "modestly and sensibly in seemly apparel, not with braided hair or gold or pearls or costly attire but by good deeds" (RSV). Women of his day did go in for elaborate hairdos. Some braided their hair with gold thread and jewels. Others dyed it, powdered it with gold or added blond hair imported from the Germanic tribes. Many wore wigs. This caused quite a problem for the Pharisees in determining, for the purposes of Sabbath keeping, what part of a woman's attire was apparel and what part was an ornament which constituted an unnecessary Sabbath burden. In the Talmud we find this ruling:

A woman may go out on the Sabbath [in the courtyard of her house only] wearing plaits of hair, whether of her own hair or of another woman or of an animal; or with frontlets or other kinds of ornaments sewn to her headgear; or with a hairnet or false curl, or with wadding in her ear or shoe or prepared for a sanitary purpose.

Some of the Greek mystery religions had regulations about women's dress similar to those in the New Testament. One inscription reads: "A consecrated woman shall not have gold ornaments, nor rouge, nor face-whitening, nor head-band, nor braided hair, nor shoes, except those made of felt or the skins of sacred animals."

Even the British Parliament tried proscribing women's adornments. In 1770 it enacted the following:

All women of whatever age, rank, profession, or degree, who shall after this act, impose upon or seduce and betray into matrimony any of His Majesty's subjects, by virtue of scents, paints, or cosmetics, artificial teeth, false hair, Spanish wool, iron stays, bolstered hips, or high-heeled shoes, shall incur the penalty of the law now in force against witchcraft and like misdemeanors, and the marriage under such circumstances shall be null and void.

In comparison to this the scriptural limits are mild indeed, yet surprisingly not one commentator I have read is in favor of taking them literally. One pontificates that pearls and other adornments are "not to be understood as any further prohibited than they are inconsistent with seemly apparel." W. M. Stratham in *The Pulpit Commentary* seems to go even further from Paul's view:

As God is the God of beauty, and nature is clothed with the garments of glory and beauty, so here we have the true idea carried out in religion. Women are "to adorn themselves," God's most beautiful work in creation, the human frame, is to be fitly apparelled: for to this day art knows no higher subject than the human face and form. But—modesty is to be the spirit of all adornment.

Martin Luther, I am told, said that if a husband desires a wife to adorn herself she should do so.

I am still not completely persuaded, and do not remember ever buying myself any jewelry except two one-dollar necklaces to coordinate some colors in my clothes. But judging by Christmas and birthday presents through the years, my family and Christian friends are convinced I need a little sparkle added to my seemly apparel.

Peter also has ideas on what constitutes the best-dressed woman. He states, "Let not yours be the outward adorning with braiding of hair, decoration of gold, and wearing of [expensive?] robes, but let it be the hidden person of the heart with the imperishable jewel of a gentle [meek] and quiet spirit, which in God's sight is very precious" (1 Pet. 3:3-4, RSV). So it may begin to seem that we do have part of a blueprint for the ideal woman. Good works are the outcome of the new birth in any person, however, and both Peter and Paul elsewhere exhort *men* to be meek and self-controlled in the face of unjustified criticism and ill-treatment. Meekness was Moses' great characteristic. Christ proclaimed himself meek and lowly in heart and also declared

"Blessed are the meek" when addressing his male disciples. We cannot regard these qualities as uniquely required of female Christians, therefore; rather, they are the Lord's ideal for every believer.

Few commentators claim that Paul's restrictions apply to what a woman was to wear in church, although the whole paragraph has often been labeled "Instructions for Worship." No doubt this is because what Paul described as the desirable "adorning" of women would hardly be limited to worship time. It was to have modesty, sobriety (meaning not a long face but "habitual inner self-government," as one scholar puts it) and good works rather than expensive clothing and jewelry. This is an area where many women in Western evangelical churches have departed somewhat from the apostolic pattern; and the lady in Proverbs was certainly expensively attired. So it seems to most men that this is a relative matter, perhaps depending on the family income and the husband's wishes. But let us not forget the positive side of the apostolic patterns and the importance of the adornment of the inner woman.

9
PRAYING AND PROPHESYING WITH COVERED HEAD

Probably the logical consideration after ornaments and clothing is Paul's discourse in 1 Corinthians 11 in which, according to the AV, he says, "Every woman that prayeth or prophesieth with her head uncovered dishonoureth her head: for that is even all one as if she were shaven" (v. 5).

I have spent long hours considering this difficult passage. If Paul had just said, "God wants all women to have their heads covered when they pray and prophesy," and left it at that, there would be no problem. Instead, he precedes and follows the above statement with various arguments, the logic of which is difficult to discern. For instance, to be shaved does not in the least seem the same as having a head full of uncovered hair. But we had better look at the whole passage:

(2) Now I praise you, brethren, that ye remember me in all things,

and keep the ordinances ["traditions," ASV and others] as I deliv-
ered them to you. (3) But I would have you know that the head of
every man is Christ; and the head of the woman is the man; and the
head of Christ is God. (4) Every man praying or prophesying, hav-
ing his head covered, dishonoureth his head. (5) But every woman
that prayeth or prophesieth with her head uncovered dishonoureth
her head: for that is even all one as if she were shaven. (6) For if
the woman be not covered, let her also be shorn: but if it be a shame
for a woman to be shorn or shaven, let her be covered. (7) For a
man indeed ought not to cover his head, forasmuch as he is the
image and glory of God: but the woman is the glory of man. (8) For
the man is not of the woman; but the woman of the man. (9) Neither
was the man created for the woman; but the woman for the man.
(10) For this cause ought the woman to have power on her head be-
cause of the angels. (11) Nevertheless, neither is the man without
the woman, neither the woman without the man, in the Lord. (12)
For as the woman is of the man, even so is the man also by the wom-
an; but all things of God. (13) Judge in yourselves: is it comely that
a woman pray unto God uncovered? (14) Doth not even nature
itself teach you, that, if a man have long hair, it is a shame unto
him? (15) But if a woman have long hair, it is a glory to her: for her
hair is given her for a covering. (16) But if any man seem to be
contentious, we have no such custom, neither the churches of God.
(1 Cor. 11:2-16)

Perplexities in Paul's Arguments If a covering on her
head signifies that a woman is "under the power of her husband" as the AV margin suggests, why wouldn't a covering
on a man's head appropriately indicate his subjection to
God? And what about an unmarried woman? Who is her
head? Isn't any woman believer a part of the church of
Christ, whose head he is (Col. 2:18)? Conversely, God is
called the husband of his people in the Old Testament, and

the church (men and women collectively) the bride of Christ in the New. So again, why shouldn't all Christians have their heads covered to demonstrate this relationship?

Next comes the argument that since Adam was created first and then the woman from and for him she should show her subjection to him. Yet Adam was the only man to be "before" the woman. Every other man has been born from and extremely dependent for a time on a woman, as Paul suddenly remembers; and the inconsistency of his previous statements seems to strike him in verses 11 and 12. He then invites his audience to judge for themselves, a suggestion which perhaps is a helpful hint for us today.

Then, too, it is not clear if Paul wants all women to be veiled all the time in a worship service, or only married women, or only the women who pray and prophesy while they are in the act of doing that. Perhaps such women had begun to remove their veils for just that purpose so that they might be heard more clearly.

What really is his main reason for advocating this covering? Is it for God's sake? I grew up in a denomination where all girls and women wore hats in church, and the purpose seemed to be to show reverence for God. Even women tourists were required to cover their heads while sightseeing in the church whether a service was in progress or not. Or was it rather to demonstrate male headship for man's own satisfaction? I have found some commentators who implied so: "Before man, the lord of creation, woman must have her head covered at worship, since that is the proper way for her to recognize the divine order at creation." Or was it for another, quite unexpected reason?

In the midst of his argument Paul puts this puzzling sentence: "For this cause ought the woman to have power on her head because of the angels." At first this left me cold.

I care very much whether I am pleasing to the Lord, and do not want in any way to offend fellow believers or the unconverted; but must I consider the angels also? For a moment it seemed almost comical to imagine angels peering down at some of the monstrosities which in our western countries have gone by the name of ladies' hats. In fact, each time I came on furlough from the Orient I found these "creations" very distracting in church and usually sat near the front to avoid having them in eye range. Surely these were not what Paul had in mind as coverings! And could the church today be at fault for almost entirely neglecting the angels with whom Peter also seemed well-acquainted?

Paul then jumps from the argument for women's heads being covered to the merits of short and long hair for men and women, and here this rather ambiguous statement appears: "Doesn't nature itself teach that for a man to wear long hair is degrading?" We have a double problem here. First, how long is *long*? Paul did not always wear his hair very short, for Acts 18:18 tells us that at Cenchreae he had his hair cut short because he was under a vow. Second, what is meant by *nature*? In the animal world it is often the male which has the longer hair or feathers, for example, lions, peacocks and roosters.

Furthermore, if left to "nature," a man's hair usually grows as long and beautiful as a woman's, as has been seen in the hippie culture. And if long hair in men is objectionable to God, why were the Nazarites forbidden to cut theirs? And why did God tell Aaron and his sons to wear "bonnets" when they entered the tabernacle if men's uncovered heads are to the glory of God? Paul himself seems to end up conscious that his reasoning may not have been too convincing, for he says that if there are those who still want to argue about the matter all he can say is that this is the custom in the existing churches.

With such confused thoughts I obviously needed help from the commentators. It was a comfort to find that as conservative a scholar as Donald Guthrie speaks of "the usual Pauline abruptness, digressions, and . . . habit of losing the line of his argument altogether." J. S. Glen notes the peculiarity of Paul's arguments in this passage, including his appeal to custom and nature, which "does not reflect the Paul who in the high points of doctrinal interpretation exhibits the richest evangelical insight. The extremity of tone suggests an urgency to be met more than an issue to be clarified." Actually, there are nearly as many views on this passage as there are commentators, and we will now consider some in detail.

Conventions of That Day   *The Pulpit Commentary* contains quite a wide range of views from that of David Thomas— "There are some things in these verses that perhaps no one can rightly interpret, and that may have been written from personal opinion rather than Divine inspiration"—to that of C. Lipcomb, who professes great admiration for Paul's arguments, claiming he is outstanding among the apostles for his "insight into the natural economy of the universe."

Both here and elsewhere few care to comment on hair length, but all agree that the "covering" Paul speaks about is a veil. I wondered why the church had changed from this to hats until I found that Calvin in one place refers to the veil as "the badge of celibacy," so I suspect it is because of both Moslem and Roman Catholic use of the veil that Protestants have eschewed it. Most commentators assume that a veil was used by Corinthian women as a token of marriage. Some would have it that all Greek women wore veils, others that only the wealthy did; some say there were two kinds of veils, a long one covering face and bust, worn in exceptional circumstances (mourning, marriage, going on a dangerous journey), and a more common short one, worn the rest of the time, concealing hair, ears and forehead only.

According to J. V. Fitzmeyer women could be present at Greek religious assemblies bareheaded, and thus Christian women were not innovating when they attended Christian gatherings without a head covering. Others believe that at some pagan altars women did cover their heads. However, there were one thousand priestess prostitutes at the temple of Aphrodite in Corinth, and some say that they, and also slaves, were forbidden to wear veils on pain of torture. So perhaps Paul wanted no confusion to arise between these and the Christian women, and therefore decreed synagogue tradition should be followed in the Christian churches. After all, the Corinthian church was already involved in drunkenness and gluttony at their "love feasts" (as mentioned next in 1 Cor. 11), and with unveiled women present outsiders might expect even greater debauchery. This would not explain, however, why Paul seems to limit the veil-wearing to women praying and prophesying, unless they alone had begun to remove them for that reason.

The Bible nowhere else states that women must be veiled and here again we find commentators not quite agreeing on what the biblical custom was. One says that "young girls were more apt to be veiled than married women," but most state that married women were always covered.

Another suggestion is that their new emancipation had gone to the heads of the Christian women and they had discarded their veils as a sign of independence from their husbands. Others even suggest that some of the women had shaved their heads in order to obliterate sex differences in view of Galatians 3:28. One of the chief problems in the passage, however, is the uncertainty about whether Paul is referring to men and women in general or to a wife's relationship to her husband. Personally I think the latter meaning is the most likely. However, we will limit ourselves here to the matter of women having their heads covered to pray and prophesy.

The Power on the Woman's Head   If Paul were only concerned that Jewish or Greek customs not be hastily overthrown, would he have added verse 10, "For this cause ought the woman to have power on her head because of the angels"? I found some interesting and surprising explanations for this difficult verse. One honest and brave man, David Thomas, wrote, "Who shall divine the meaning of verse 10? . . . To me it is utterly incomprehensible." Those who can only think in terms of male headship twist this word *power* to mean *under* the power of another, as the AV margin states. This word is used sixty-six times in the New Testament, however, always in the sense of power of choice and liberty of doing as one pleases. It is the word Paul used earlier in this same letter concerning a wife and husband's each having power over the other's body (7:4) and also in the admonition "Take heed lest by any means this *liberty* of yours becomes a stumbling block to them that are weak" (8:9). No classical writer uses it in any other sense than this.

Sir William Ramsey in his *Cities of St. Paul* states in this connection: "Most of the ancient and modern commentators say the 'authority' which the woman wears on her head is the authority to which she is subject—a preposterous idea which a Greek scholar would laugh at anywhere except in the New Testament where (as they seem to think) Greek words may mean anything that the commentators choose."

John Lightfoot also believes the woman's own authority is meant here.

With this in mind, Jane A. McNally in *The Place of Woman in the New Testament Church* comes up with a novel idea. She views the construction of the whole passage as being comparable to a teeter-totter, verse 10 being the point of balance: Women have the authority, as each sees fit, to choose whether to veil at worship or not. "One end of the see-saw is her obligation not to bring dishonor to her husband by appearing in the guise of a harlot (3-9); and the other her right to pray to God unveiled (11-15)." When the proprieties are such that they weight the former end heavily, Paul would advise her to make her decision in the light of verse 6, which is meant to express what public opinion might say.

Some commentators who admit that grammatically this word *exousia* means "power" and not a sign of someone else's authority mention a view held down the centuries from some of the early fathers and rabbis, namely, that women need "power," or a veil with magic properties, as protection against the evil angels who would try to seduce them. This idea is based on Genesis 6, but since Christ said the angels neither marry nor are given in marriage (Mt. 22:30) presumably they have neither sex organs nor urges. This is the view expressed in the Talmud regarding good angels, whereas evil spirits can propagate themselves! In any case, two commentators point out that Paul only used this particular term for good angels, and most assume that it refers to those angels thought by the Jews to be present at public worship. "Angels are delegated special duties, and one of them is . . . in connection with prayer. It was said: 'After all the places of worship have completed their services, the angel who is appointed over prayers gathers up all the devotions which had been offered in all the places of worship, forms them into crowns and sets them upon the head of the Holy One' " (Exod. R. xxl.4).

A further suggestion is that "the angels" refer to the seraphim who, out of reverence, veil their faces with their wings in God's presence. But if women and seraphim are to be veiled, why not men, since, according to the psalmist and the writer to the Hebrews, they are at present a little lower than the angels?

Another interesting but complicated view has recently been advanced by Dick and Joyce Boldrey in an article in *Trinity Studies*. They note that Paul makes use of the pun in his various references to "head." Also the Greek *exousia* ("power") in some ancient texts reads *kalumma,* the Arabic word for "veil," the root of which is a common verb meaning "to have power, dominion over," and thus is the equivalent of the Greek word *exousia.* They state: "We opt that Paul used the combined meaning, and may have left the word in Aramaic, as is suggested by Tertullian's citations of verse 10, one time translated 'power,' another 'veil.' . . . So the *veil* which symbolizes the effacement of man's (humanity's) glory in the presence of God, at the same time serves as a sign of the *exousia* [power] which is given to the woman."

The Boldreys then conclude,
Paul used the physical symbols "head" and "veil" to convey two spiritual realities. The first is that human beings are created not in their own image but God's, and should therefore show his glory, not their own, when they worship. The second is that in Christ males are not superior to females; they both have "power on their heads" to worship God. For "we all, with unveiled face, reflecting the glory of the Lord, are being changed into his image from glory to glory. . . . For God . . . has shined in our hearts to give the light of the knowledge of the glory of God in the face of Christ." (2 Cor. 4:6)

Tentative Conclusions Merely reading English translations of 1 Corinthians 11 would hardly enable one to reach a conclusion like the Boldreys'. Is there anything in the text itself which can guide us without our having all this background knowledge?

The fact that Paul refers to tradition, nature and custom, and invites readers to "judge in themselves" ("judge for yourselves," NASB) seems ground for regarding his instructions here as something not necessarily binding on us today. One writer notes that 1 Corinthians is the only letter where Paul does not seem quite sure of himself. Paul admits that one or two of his judgments lack the authority of a clear ruling by Jesus, and although Paul believes he interprets the Spirit's wisdom he will not go beyond the phrases "but in my judgment" and "I think I have the Spirit of God." Although Paul does not use those phrases in the passage we are considering, most commentators agree that the wearing of a veil concerns a custom of dress which was merely local and temporary.

That it was more than mere custom among the Jews, at least at some period between the first century B.C. and the sixth century A.D., is evident from a study of the Talmud. For a Jewish wife to be seen in the street with her head uncovered was grounds for divorce without even the return of the marriage settlement money, a usual provision for women in the case of divorce for less heinous reasons.

The following have their marriage dissolved without receiving what is due them under their Kethubar: a woman who transgresses Jewish law, such as going into public with uncovered head, spinning in the street or conversing with all sorts of men; a woman who curses her husband's children in his presence; a loud-voiced woman, which means one who talks in her house and her neighbors can hear what she says. (Keth. vii. 6)

There is also a footnote to say that at marriage a bride covered her hair and it was considered immodest for her to expose it. Cohen also explains that the ordinary term for marriage is *Kiddushin* denoting "sanctification." It is so called because "the husband prohibits his wife to the whole world like an object which is dedicated to the sanctuary." On the other side of the coin, the penalty for anyone else uncovering a woman's head in the market place was 400 zuz, equal to 100 temple shekels.

Joachim Jeremias in *Jerusalem in the Time of Jesus* tells us there were women so strict that they did not even uncover their heads in the house:

Women like Quimhit, who, it was said, saw seven sons admitted to the high priesthood, which was regarded as divine reward for her extreme propriety: "May it (this and that) befall me if the beams of my house have ever seen the hair of my head." Only in her wedding procession was a bride seen with uncovered head, and then only if she were a virgin, not a widow.

If these conditions prevailed in Paul's time, one can readily understand his acute uneasiness that some women were removing their veils to pray and prophesy. We should remember, too, that he had ended the previous chapter with the words, "So whether you eat or drink or whatever you do, do it all for the glory of God. Do not cause anyone to stumble, whether Jews, Greeks, or the church of God—even as I try to please everybody in every way. For I am not seeking my own good but the good of many, so that they may be saved" (1 Cor. 10:31-33, NIV).

Julian McPheeters points out this:

Although the problems in the Corinthian church may seem far removed from those in the present day church, Paul solves them by principles which are eternal. One of these has to do with accommodating one's teaching and preaching, within limits, to the habits and customs of the people in order that the fullest impact of the Gospel message may be realized.

"Women in matters of dress should conform to the demands and usage of the public sentiment of the community" is the way Hodge sums it up. (Would he still stick by that today, I wonder, when "anything goes" in most communities?) So, if women's hair in Palestine and at Corinth was considered unseemly, by all means cover it up. In Japan, the back of a woman's neck was for a long time considered sexually stimulating. Forty years ago in certain parts of China, to see a woman's naked foot or her arm above the elbow was thought immoral.

Incidentally, most Chinese women did not wear hats, while the men did. And in the early days of missionary work that great pioneer, Hudson Taylor, felt that missionary men should wear the pigtail required of Chinese men by their Manchu rulers, in spite of Paul's remarks in this passage. This was certainly along the lines of Paul's determination to be all things to all men that he might "by all means save some."

Campbell Morgan wisely states,
As we study this passage, let us beware of the slavery of tradition. Beware lest we let something important in the long ago govern our thinking in the present time. Yet let us remember the possible importance of secondary things, because the church is ever witnessing to the world.

With this in mind, when we arrived home on our last furlough, I reluctantly parted with the necessary dollars to purchase a hat. On Sunday morning when I appeared with it on, after years in the Orient without one, my husband's reaction was, *"Boy*, you look funny!" Needless to say, I happily followed the present custom at home and have not worn one since.

A New Interpretation   Such had been the state of my best thinking on the topic until I read an article in a recent issue of the *Westminster Theological Journal* which throws considerable new light on the theme of this chapter. Since it appears to make Paul's words in this passage much more logical and unified, I feel some of it must be included, although it is difficult to summarize a thirty-page article without doing injustice to the scholarship behind it.

The main point of the writer, James B. Hurley, is that the real Greek meaning of verse 5 is not covered hair, but loosened hair. He tells us there is little information available to us about veiling customs in the early church. The Greek pottery which shows elaborate hairstyles and no head covering dates well before Christ. The Talmud stretched over seven centuries so we cannot now be sure what customs were current in Paul's day. Moslems introduced veiling after the writing of the Koran, which was well after the New Testament era, and may have influenced Jewish custom. Jewish men wore a long rectangular mantle with the ends over the arms of the wearer, and this shawl, or Tallith, was "spread as a sign of reverence over the head of the Jewish man when he prayed. . . . The purpose was that the person might 'appear white before God.' "

Was Paul trying to do away with this custom when he speaks of it being dishonoring for a man to pray covered (11:4)? Hurley says the Greek (*kata kephales echon*) does not contain the word *shawl* or *covering*. The only time Paul uses this word is in verse 15 where the Greek word *anti* has usually been translated "for" or "as" instead of given its usual meaning of "instead of." To give its full meaning the verse should read, "A woman's hair is a divinely given sign of her role. Her hair is given her instead of a shawl or veil."

As for the word in verse 5 describing the woman, which

has always been translated with the idea of being uncovered or unveiled, Hurley says it is the same root word as the Septuagint uses in Leviticus 13:45 to describe the leper whose disease has been diagnosed: "He shall let his hair hang loose" as a warning to people of his uncleanness; and also in Numbers 5:18, where a woman accused of adultery was to have "her hair loosed" (RV), or "let down" (Berkeley), thus being set apart from the community until proved innocent or guilty. If innocent, her hair was put up again, if guilty (since in New Testament times the Jews did not have power to inflict capital punishment), she had her head shaved.

Hurley claims that if women were really veiled as supposed, there would have been no need for Paul and Peter to speak against gold-braided hair, for it would not have shown. The custom at that time, begun with the dancing girls, was to put the hair in from eleven to twenty-one braids, with a teardrop or tiny circle of gold every inch or so down the length of the braids, creating a striking shimmer of gold with every movement. The fact that both apostles prohibit this indicates it had already appeared in the churches. Hurley thinks, therefore, that most women were worshiping without veils, but wearing their hair up, pinning or folding the braids on top or at the back of their heads as was done at their marriage.

I had already seen in *Manners and Customs of Bible Lands* that a bride on her way to the bridegroom's house allowed her hair to be loose and flowing, but on arrival older women arranged it, presumably in this marital style. But contrary to Hurley's view the author of that book states that the flowing locks were hidden under a thick veil. "From this time on custom would dictate that her face was not to be unveiled in public."

Hurley points out that Paul had earlier chided the Corinthians for thinking they were already "reigning" with Christ; and probably some of the women, on the ground of Christ's words that in the resurrection they neither marry nor are given in marriage and Paul's words that in Christ there is neither male nor female, had let their hair loose or down thereby to proclaim their new status.

He suggests this would horrify some in the congregation, leading to a controversy in which both a "hair-up" party and a "loosened hair" party might cite Paul for support. "One can envision a [third] party arising which would advocate wearing the shawl. . . . In the midst of this controversy Paul was asked his opinion. . . . He would not want to alienate any but rather win all parties to his side."

So Paul begins his argument from a hierarchy—God, Christ, man, woman. Thus any man praying with his hair done up like a woman dishonors himself by indicating he is under the authority of a man and dishonors Christ whom he should reflect in his relation to his own wife, that is, "Christ is dishonored when one who should be under none save Himself and God publicly proclaims that a man is over him."

As to the wife, the husband would be dishonored in his wife's rejection of his authority; she would also dishonor herself by loosening her hair, for she thus would put on herself the public sign of an accused adulteress. This would be the equivalent of a confession and therefore she should be shaven. "Paul is concerned that in the midst of a woman's exercising the gifts of prayer and prophecy . . . she must continue to maintain her proper relation to her husband." But what about women being co-heirs with Christ (1 Pet. 3:7) some might ask? Paul answers this in verses 10-12, Hurley tells us.

Like others, Hurley recognizes the difficulties of verse 10, but agrees with Ramsey that it refers to a woman's own authority. His proposition is that Paul refers to angels four times in this letter, in each case in connection with problems at Corinth. In 6:1 he had said that Christians will judge both the world and angels in the future reign with Christ (so why couldn't they settle problems among themselves satisfactorily now?). The Corinthians had thought themselves already equal with the angels, showing no sexual distinctions, speaking with tongues of angels (13:1). The divinely structured hierarchy places women under the husband's authority but of no other being.

It is as we consider the exalted place of women within the order of creation, together with the Corinthian boast of their relation to the angels that we come to a proper understanding of Paul's remark in 11:10 . . . which marks a transition in Paul's development. Having stressed the subordination of woman within the marital relation, Paul moved to develop a more positive side.

Hurley then states that a woman's hair marks her as a woman; its style marks her either as accepting her role in creation or rejecting it. The biblical place of woman (unlike that of most pagan societies) is above all of creation, barring her husband. The hair done up on her head

must therefore be understood as a sign of tremendous authority, as well as a sign of a particular relationship to her husband . . . a sign of her proper authority as vice-regent with her husband over the rest of creation; it marks her as a woman, part of mankind, and over the angels. That Paul's word is surprising in this context which had previously stressed subordination is no doubt to be interpreted as part of his design . . . sympathetically apologetic, designed to win women to obedience.

In verses 11 and 12 Paul develops the theme of the interrelatedness of men and women. Though God had designed an "economic subordination" for women, this does not mean men are independent and women dependent; rather, they are mutually dependent. "At creation women were in one sphere equal with men, and in another subordinate. In the initiation of the new creation they were equal with their husbands in the sphere of charismatic gifts, and subordinate within the family sphere."

Hurley then concludes that Paul would thus address himself to the three parties back in Corinth:

You asked me to judge whether it is proper that a woman pray to God uncovered. I've told you enough that you can . . . judge for yourselves. God's plan in nature shows you the way. A man is shamed if he has long hair, while that same long hair brings glory to a woman. You can see that hair is given to be a sign of the distinction between men and women. This natural sign of long hair is also sufficient covering and there is no need for a shawl.

If anyone still wants to argue about the need for a covering, he should know that neither we nor the churches of God have any other custom than that women should pray and prophesy with their heads covered . . . by their hair.

As already noted, this view of Hurley's does make for a more unified argument in this whole passage. One criticism might be that, like many others, this author, while mostly speaking of the husband and wife relationship, in a few places seems to apply his ideas to all men and all women. Also it is hard to see why Christ is dishonored if a man appears to be under the authority of another man. In this temporal world many men are in positions of subordination to employers.

It is confusing, and a little irritating, to find such divergent views about how a woman is to appear in church. I must confess to having to resist a small initial impulse to think, "A plague on both of you, translators and commentators!" But we should appreciate those who have given themselves to understanding the original languages of the Scriptures, and pray that there will be more who approach them with an open mind and not with preconceived ideas and wishful thinking, more who can fully evaluate the possibilities in the original words of the writers.

As I ponder what the Lord really does want of women with regard to praying and prophesying with covered heads, my most reassuring thought has been the verse, "Man looketh on the outward appearance, but God looketh on the heart" (1 Sam. 16:7). Men do judge by outward appearance, and so to a certain extent we should govern ourselves by this for the sake of the gospel.

If one woman feels, however, that this passage in 1 Corinthians as found in most translations is binding on her, and out of loving obedience to the Lord she covers her head to pray and prophesy, surely he will accept it as from her heart. And if another truly loves the Lord, and with no idea of disrespect and no desire to draw attention to herself in a land of bareheads or to waste precious money on silly hats, prays and speaks uncovered, will God not judge her by her heart and not her head?

Does God really desire to see the good old Salvation Army or missionary "bun" or other long-haired style on wives or on all adult women? Or is it enough for us to give adequate indication that we are women and not men and that our heart's desire is to please him? One cannot help feeling that if the matter were really of vital importance he would have made sure there was no possibility of mistaking his preference.

10
WOMAN IN CHURCH

Perhaps more important than her dress and headcovering is the question of a woman's conduct in church. Looking first at 1 Corinthians 14:33-35 we read,

(33) For God is not the author of confusion, but of peace, as in all churches of the saints. (34) Let your women keep silence in the churches: for it is not permitted unto them to speak; but they are commanded to be under obedience, as also saith the law. (35) And if they will learn any thing, let them ask their husbands at home: for it is a shame for women to speak in the church.

In English, and taken in isolation, these verses seem quite clear. Yet just before, in chapter 11, Paul had gone into great detail about why women should have either their heads covered or their hair up when they pray and prophesy. Would he waste time on this discussion if he was soon to tell them they must not prophesy at all? So think some commentators. Others, however, insist that after "further re-flection" Paul changed his view!

We must remember, too, that both the prophet Joel and the apostle Peter had said, "And it shall come to pass in the last days, saith God, I will pour out my Spirit upon all flesh: and your sons and your *daughters shall prophesy,* . . . and on my servants and on my *handmaidens* I will pour out in those days of my Spirit; and they *shall prophesy*" (Acts 2:17-18). Was Paul contradicting them?

How thankful I am for Peter's word that in Paul's letters "are some things hard to be understood." I certainly have no wish to be among the "unlearned and unstable who wrest the scriptures to their destruction," but have earnestly and prayerfully tried to find out (1) if Paul meant exactly what the English translation seems to say, (2) if there is a reasonable explanation for the apparent contradiction and (3) if there is a legitimate reason for some of the things commonly done by Christian women today, particularly on the mission field, which seem contrary to some of Paul's injunctions. Some tentative conclusions from this search will be recorded in the next few chapters.

What Is an Official Church Service?   Turning to the com-mentaries for light, I found one which recognized that the gift of prophecy is given to women but said it is only meant to be exercised in private. Yet in 1 Corinthians 11 Paul talks about disorderliness at the communion service and uses the expression, "when ye come together in the church." The AV heads the whole chapter "Rules for divine worship" while various commentaries similarly use such expressions as "Conduct in Public Worship."

Another commentator suggests that the passage about women praying and prophesying does not refer to "official services in the church." But what exactly was "an official service" in New Testament times? Paul describes one in chapter 14: "When ye come together, every one of you hath a psalm, hath a doctrine, hath a tongue, hath a revelation, hath an interpretation. . . . If any man speak in an unknown tongue, let it be by two, or at the most by three. . . . Let the prophets speak two or three. . . . For ye may all prophesy one by one, that all may learn, and all may be comforted" (1 Cor. 14:26-27, 29, 31). That is certainly different from most official church services today. In fact, it seems a very informal type of fellowship meeting and therefore all the more strange if a woman with the gift of prophecy must be silent there.

Another (an Episcopalian) states, "It is evident that in this primitive Christian worship great freedom was allowed." But gradually the churches "advanced" to abolishing free prayer, limiting participation in the service to a presiding minister. That this must be a man was, of course, a foregone conclusion to him.

What Kind of Speaking Did Paul Mean?   The most important clue to solving the problem of the apparent contradiction is the meaning of the Greek word translated "speak" in 14:34. Typical of most commentators, who judge only by the western form of church service, is one who notes that "of course it is public speaking which is here intended, as the context implies."

The translators of the NEB were evidently of that opinion and thought to clarify the matter by saying that "women should not address the meeting. They have no licence to speak, but should keep their place as the law directs. If there is something they want to know they should ask their husbands at home. It is a shocking thing that a woman should address the congregation."

Campbell Morgan, however, points out that this Greek word (*laleo*) is used over three hundred times in the New Testament, usually with the sense of talking, chattering, questioning, arguing; and he feels that that is the meaning with which Paul is using it here. Since Paul begins with the thought about confusion, and tells the wives to ask their husbands at home if they have any questions, this seems a much more likely meaning than if he is interjecting the matter about asking questions at home into the middle of instruction about not addressing the congregation. A friend who works among Jewish people says that even today he has often heard the president of a synagogue bang on the pulpit and shout to the women's section to be quiet.

Julian C. McPheeters says,

Another disorder in the worship of the Corinthian church, besides the tongues problem, was the disturbance made by the wives talking in undertones to their husbands. Women were not subject to education in the ancient pagan world. Although the Greeks had the highest standard of culture, they did not educate their women. Wives were dependent on their husbands for knowledge. The talkativeness of women in church called for disciplinary measures. The women are directed to seek at home the information they desire. Contrary to the pronouncements of some, Paul here says not one word against women's participating in the service of worship.

In a Jewish synagogue the women are seated separately. We do not know if this custom carried over into the Christian meetings at first and therefore whether the women were whispering to their husbands or to each other. Certainly in early church history they were seated separately. In pre-war China, too, women and men sat on opposite sides of the church. And since in most pagan religions there is little sense of worshipful reverence and since most of the women of inland China were illiterate, it was natural that in the young churches, when much that was entirely new to the people was preached, there was murmuring and questioning—not to mention children and dogs running around, babies being breast-fed and even peddlers coming in looking for customers.

To further illustrate the kind of situation quite unthinkable to anyone who knows nothing but a western church building, I remember my shock at an incident one Sunday morning at the beginning of the typhoid season early in my career in China. The church in our city had been bombed flat the previous year by the Japanese, and the Christians were meeting in a rented upstairs room. In the course of the service a dear old Chinese elder announced that a Christian doctor and two nurses had walked in from the military hospital, two miles away, to give innoculations. So at the close of the worship service, while the baptized believers had communion at the front of the room, the inquirers and children were to get their shots at the back. Just a few benches separated the two groups.

While there was much more justification for this procedure than for the scandalous behavior of some of the Corinthians at their communion services, I think it illustrates how entirely different the concept of worship in most of the pagan world is from that of centuries-old western churches (which is all that most commentators have experienced). So it is highly possible that it was about chattering and lack of outward reverence on the part of the newly converted Corinthian women that Paul was speaking here. Donald Guthrie also holds this view.

Another possibility, to which the Boldreys subscribe, is that since the word *laleo* has already been used two dozen times in this chapter in connection with *glossai*—the two words together referring to "babbling" in tongues—the meaning is the same in the two verses about women (vv. 34-35). Paul has twice before, in 14:28 and 30, said that people should "keep silent" when confusion would otherwise occur from several people wanting to speak at once, and this is a continuation of the same idea. Paul is not implying that these men are to remain silent forever, but only when their speaking would constitute an interruption.

Are There Other Explanations?   In the Codex Bezae and in some other early manuscripts the verses about women keeping silent appear at the *end* of chapter 14 or else as a marginal gloss. Some even regard it as "an interpolation by a later hand," probably at the end of the first century when women were being downgraded by the church fathers. Moffatt suggests that messengers from Corinth, who were troubled by the women's behavior there, asked Paul to add the item to his letter! Since there is no manuscript which omits these verses completely, however, we assume their authenticity.

Some suggest that verses 33 and 34 are actually a quotation from a letter the Judaizers at Corinth wrote to Paul. In fact, Coneybeare and Howson use quotation marks for about twenty verses in 1 Corinthians, and Sir William Ramsey states, "We should be ready to suspect Paul is making a quotation from a letter addressed to him by the Corinthians when he alludes to their 'knowledge' or when any statement stands in marked contrast either with the immediate context, or with Paul's own known views."

Some neatly dodge the issue by saying that the gift of prophecy ceased after the New Testament Scriptures were complete and therefore the question of women prophesying is now irrelevant. Such an idea of prophecy is rather limited, however, and seems different from Paul's. Earlier in chapter 14, in explaining the superiority of prophesying over speaking in tongues, Paul says, "He that prophesieth speaketh . . . to edification, and exhortation, and comfort. He that speaketh in an unknown tongue edifieth himself; but he that prophesieth edifieth the *church*" (vv. 3-4). Surely the church in every age needs edification, exhortation and comfort. (Also, if prophecy is meant to edify the church, it would be pointless for women to exercise the gift in private.) It would be strange, too, for the Holy Spirit to cause Paul to tell the Corinthian believers to "desire spiritual gifts, but rather that ye may prophesy" (14:1) if this gift was soon to be taken away. Martyn Lloyd-Jones says about prophecy, "Prophets actually taught the law and applied and interpreted it, in addition to foretelling." Others hold a similar view. Furthermore, Peter at Pentecost had claimed that they were now in "the last days" in which God had promised through Joel that he would send his Spirit on all flesh, men and women alike, and they would prophesy. Since Christ has not yet returned, aren't we still in those "last days"?

James Hurley explains away the apparent contradiction by referring back to 14:29, which reads in the NEB, "Of the prophets, two or three may speak, while the rest exercise their judgment upon what is said. . . . It is for prophets to control prophetic inspiration." Women could certainly prophesy but were not to take part in discussing and evaluating the messages to explore their meaning and make sure they were not contrary to the true gospel. That would be "assuming the anomalous role of judging men . . . [a] violation of created authority structure." It is hard to see why, if the Holy Spirit were indeed poured out on men and women, the resulting utterances had to be examined so critically, but evidently Paul had found he could not trust everyone who claimed to be guided by the Spirit. One would think the Spirit could give women as well as men true discernment, but perhaps Paul felt that they had little scriptural background as well as that it is insufferable for a man to be criticized by a woman. Evidently the male believers did not appreciate this from each other either, for a professional ministry soon eliminated any opportunity for public sermon evaluation.

Others have a similar idea that the women Paul refers to were merely wanting to take part in discussion, something men sometimes did in the synagogues. Jean Héring in his commentary states,

There was no question therefore of imposing silence on women who spoke in a state of inspiration to deliver a message. This contingency is expressly dealt with and passed as permissible in 11:5 where women were ordered to have their heads covered, and no exegete has ever doubted that the point there concerns women speaking in church gatherings. There is a clear distinction between a preaching woman who has a right to bring a message and a woman present as an ordinary member of the congregation. It goes without saying that the reason for this [partial] silence [imposed on women in the congregation] must be sought solely in a concern not to violate the rules of propriety . . . at the time. We are then in the realm of the relative. Calvin was well aware of this.

We must note that this writer says "no exegete" has doubted this. There are certainly many ordinary men who can only see in these verses an absolute and eternal divine principle that women can have no speaking ministry in the church. Calvin, however, does allow one exception. Stating that God has committed the office of teaching exclusively to men, he adds,

If anyone challenges this ruling by citing the case of Deborah and

other women of whom we are told that God at one time appointed them to govern the people, the obvious answer is that God's extra-ordinary acts do not annul the ordinary rules by which He wishes us to be bound. Thus, if at some time women held the office of prophets and teachers and were led to do so by God's spirit, He who is above all law might do this, but being an extraordinary case, it does not conflict with the constant rule.

One cannot help wondering how Calvin would determine if a woman *was* truly "led by God's spirit."

Was Paul Quoting the Oral Law?   Together with the view that this "speaking" refers to women's chattering and interrupting the service, I find the most satisfying explanation for the seeming contradiction of 1 Corinthians 11 and 14 in some information I have recently gathered concerning the oral law of the Jewish scribes which developed after Ezra's return from the captivity. Since this throws light on a number of the passages relating to women (and much more) it may be helpful to understand its origin and its impact on the Jewish mind.

For various reasons the position of Jewish women deteriorated considerably during the captivity. First, the Jews began to follow the Persian practice of seclusion of women. Second, the sex vices of the Gentiles who dominated the Jews had filled the Jewish leaders with a disgust which tended to extend to all women. Eve's fall in Eden came to be thought of as sexual lust. Third, perhaps because women were regarded as being so frequently ceremonially unclean, during menstrual periods and after childbirth, they were not counted as part of the quorum of ten needed to establish a new synagogue or even to hold a service.

How did the synagogue originate? With the temple gone, the Jews had to find a substitute center to avert national extinction. Ezra assembled the elders of Judah a number of times, and the solution they evolved gradually became summarized in the word *Torah*, a Hebrew word meaning "teaching" or "direction." A. Cohen notes, "For the exiles it denoted the body of doctrine, *written and oral*, which had come down from past ages. . . . We may assume the Jews in Babylon had in their possession the Mosaic revelation. . . . They also had some of the prophetic writings and the Psalms."

It was the Pentateuch, however, and the oral commentaries surrounding it which were considered God's great revelation, the prophets and wisdom literature being slightly less highly regarded. Thus David says, "How I love thy Torah" (Ps. 119:97). And Ezra is described as "a ready scribe in the Torah of Moses. . . . He set his heart to seek the Torah of the Lord, and to do it, to teach the statutes and judgments" (Ezra 7:6, 10). The word translated "seek" means to deduce or interpret the text, and the majority of the teachers (scribes) who developed from Ezra's approach came to regard this system of interpretation or commentary to be as important as the text itself.

Ezra's assembly of the elders was succeeded by the Sanhedrin, composed of priests and laymen, including the scribes (later entitled *rabbis*). The Sanhedrin gradually divided into two parties. One was the Sadducees, who held a position which they regarded as fixed for all time by the written code of the Pentateuch and inseparably bound up with the temple ritual. The other, the Pharisees, held that the oral Torah was an integral part of the written Torah, enclosing it by additional precautionary measures for the purpose of avoiding unintentional infringement. Some of the Pharisees' leaders saw in the freedom of interpretation allowed by the oral law an invaluable instrument for making the Torah adaptable to varying circumstances. (It did in fact enable the Jewish religion to continue after the destruction of Herod's temple while the Sadducees faded out of existence.) However, this also laid the Pharisees open to the charge of casuistry.

Interpretation of the Torah became a science and only men who were duly qualified to expound the text could speak with authority and receive the name of *Teacher*, later *Rabbi*.

After the Exile, all the people spoke Aramaic as their first language, and most could not read the Hebrew Scriptures. (One high priest is on record as having to be read to.) Thus much of the instruction in the synagogue schools (for boys only) would be oral, and memorized by them. This instruction included both the oral and written Torah. It was probably these oral traditions Christ was referring to when he said, "Ye have heard that it was said by them of old time ... but I say unto you" (Mt. 5:21-44). Certainly "Thou shalt love thy neighbor, and hate thy enemy" was not from the Old Testament.

It was not until after the time of Christ that this oral law appeared in written form, first as the Mishnah, then as the Talmud. The latter was created as commentaries of various rabbis over a seven-hundred-year period were added together to form the Palestinian and Babylonian Talmuds, the rabbinic schools in Jerusalem and those in Alexandria each making their own compilations. Strangely, both the Mishnah and Talmud refer frequently to women, and not always in complimentary terms.

One section of the Talmud gives "the tradition of the elders" in the following way:
Women, slaves and children are exempt from the study of the law. A woman who studies the law has a reward, but not equal to the reward a man has, because she is not commanded to do so: for no one

who does anything which he is not commanded to do, receives the same reward as he who is commanded to do it, but a less one. [Curious reasoning, and almost the opposite of what Christ taught.]

Though the woman has a reward, the wise men have commanded that no man should teach his daughter the law for this reason, that the majority of women have not got a mind fitted for study, but pervert the words of the law on account of the poverty of their mind. The wise men have said "Everyone that teacheth his daughter the law is considered as if he taught her transgression." But this applies only to the oral law. As to the written law, he is not to teach her systematically; but if he has taught her, he is not to be considered as having taught her transgression.

A certain Rabbi Eleazer said, "Let the words of the law be burned rather than committed to women." It was this oral tradition which forbade women to speak in the synagogue, and it used such expressions as "It is a shame for woman to let her voice be heard among men" and "The voice of woman is as filthy nakedness." Even to hear a woman singing in private was considered unchaste.

This is very different from Old Testament practice, where many women sang God's praises and prophesied. Nowhere is there any command to women to be silent. So when Paul says, "It is not permitted unto them to speak; but they are commanded to be under obedience as also saith the law . . . for it is a shame for women to speak," he is literally quoting the oral law. The translators of the AV probably had no knowledge of this rabbinic law and in search of some justification for Paul's mention of "the law" could only come up with the suggestion of Genesis 3:16 in their marginal note. This has colored the thinking of most theologians ever since. Now that much more data on Jewish traditions and practice is available, it is easy to see that this could be the explanation for Paul's words.

In support of this, J. Stanley Glen writes,

What evidence do we have that Paul clung [to some of these tradi-tions] in spite of all that he said of the freedom which the believer has in the Gospel? ... [In silencing the women at Corinth] much as his action may have been justified in the light of local circumstances, he expects of these what any rabbi would expect of Jewish women in an ancient synagogue. For although it was probably correct that the women were indulging in ecstatic babbling, as Paul's use of the verb laleo *suggests, and that for the sake of decency and order in wor-ship they had to be restrained, the character of his injunction reflects Rabbinic practice ... "as even the law says." The law here in ques-tion is not the Pentateuch but the tradition that required women to be silent in the synagogues, and confined them to certain areas apart from men.... It was this law which, if women desired to know anything, required them to ask their husbands at home–now taken by Paul from synagogue practice and applied to Christian women in Corinth.*

Referring to the way that Paul maintains a patriarchal subordination of the woman to the man, Glen states,

Even within his Christological understanding of their interdepen-dence, an unresolved problem seems to remain. The subordination is derived not from the familiar answer previously given to irre-sponsible freedom: "All things are lawful, but not all are expedi-ent." It is derived from extrabiblical tradition that occupies a place alongside the Gospel, which is somewhat exceptional for Pauline theology.

Glen sees this as "not unlike [the position] claimed for cir-cumcision and dietary laws by his opponents in the Galatian controversy." There Paul disposed of them as "traditions." But in the case of the women

he seems to be clinging to a little of the law, which, according to his argument in Galatians and Romans, should have been overcome. This is not to say that the women in Corinth were right, and Paul wrong, only that his answer in the light of the Gospel was as yet incomplete. It had been worked out for the problem of the Jew and the Gentile, but not yet for the male and female, slave and free.

I know there are those who will say that Paul's words that "in Christ there is neither male nor female" refer only to her "spiritual privilege" of being saved, not to her "spiritual activity" or her social relationships; and also that such a view as Glen expresses threatens the doctrine of the divine inspiration of the Scriptures. With regard to the first, if the loss of distinction between sexes is spiritual, then the church, of all places, should be the place where equality exists. The second objection will be faced in the next chapter.

Meanwhile, how should God's ideal woman behave in church? Certainly she should listen in courteous silence to whoever is speaking, as do also the men of the congregation today. Also, if she is a wife and mother, she should serve no "roast preacher" to the family after a service, although if some heresy was taught she will be wise to point this out. If she has questions, she may ask her husband at home, though in these days many women have had more Bible study and done more Sunday school teaching than their husbands.

It is obvious from Paul's words in 1 Corinthians 7:13-16 that sometimes wives were Christians and husbands were not, and Peter implies the same thing in 1 Peter 3:1. From whom were these to get answers? We can be thankful that today it is not considered immodest for a woman to question the speaker afterward or to phone the minister and that a wide range of Christian books is also available.

Whether the ideal Christian woman is ever justified in opening her mouth in church in a prophetic manner or in testimony to the saving power of Christ will be considered more fully after we study another passage of Scripture.

11
WOMAN'S CHURCH ROLE: MUTE BENCHWARMER?

The other verses bearing on the conduct of women within the church are 1 Timothy 2:11-14: "(11) Let the woman learn in silence with all subjection. (12) But I suffer not a woman to teach, nor to usurp authority over the man, but to be in silence. (13) For Adam was first formed, then Eve. (14) And Adam was not deceived, but the woman being deceived was in the transgression." This English version certainly seems to limit a woman to being a perpetual benchwarmer, forever learning but never having an opportunity to pass her knowledge on, a bottomless cup never destined to overflow with the good news of Christ to others.

Paul gives no indication in these verses as to *where* women are to be "in silence." Earlier in the paragraph he says men should pray "everywhere." But he could hardly expect women to observe a continual silence in their homes and in all other places. Since he begins the paragraph with a list of prayer topics, it is usually assumed he means in some kind of Christian gathering. But is he referring to all meetings or only to that ambiguous "official church service"?

What Did the Words Originally Mean?   In most English translations Paul sounds not as if he is dealing here with the matter of chattering or babbling but as if he does not want women to do anything with their mouths, perhaps not even to sing, pray or prophesy, and certainly not to ask questions or teach. D. Edmond Hiebert, however, tells us that the word translated "silence" (*hesuchia*) has the basic meaning of quietness, tranquility, the absence of disturbance, and is the word used in 1 Timothy 2:2 for "quiet life" and in 2 Thessalonians 3:12 in the phrase "to work in quiet fashion and eat their own bread" (NASB). Therefore, he concludes, "Clearly the term does not prohibit all speech, but does call for calm, nondisruptive conduct." In other words, it is much the same idea as in 1 Corinthians 11.

Hiebert also quotes R. C. Nichol's observation that Paul here uses the word for "authoritative teaching . . . the activity of the accredited teacher, and implies the teacher's position of authority over the taught." Therefore for a woman to engage in this kind of teaching would be "a direct violation of her position of subordination."

It is not clear whether the phrase "usurping authority over the man" ("a man" or "men," according to some translations) refers to men in general or to a husband. Many commentators regard it as covering the whole male sex. Actually, the word translated "usurp authority" in the AV would more accurately be rendered "dictate to" or "domineer over." It does not suggest the idea of women snatching a prerogative given by God only to men. This word is used nowhere else in the New Testament. Originally it meant an independent actor, but it became a popular term used to indicate any autocratic personality. The quality it implies would hardly be desirable for any Christian, male or female.

If, as Hiebert suggests, the "teaching" prohibited was only that of an accredited teacher, we are given no indication by either Christ or Paul about how a Christian becomes "accredited." Possibly Paul had in mind the academic training of the scribe, which lasted a number of years before he was "ordained" a teacher and could receive the title of *Rabbi*. "Only ordained teachers transmitted and created tradition derived from the Torah which according to Pharisaic teaching ... was regarded as equal to, and indeed above, the Torah. ... Their decision had the power to bind or to loose for all time the Jews of the entire world. ... They were the guardians of a secret knowledge, of an esoteric tradition," Joachim Jeremias tells us. Certainly there were no women with such qualifications; and if that is what Paul is referring to, then it would appear that women moved by the Spirit could still prophesy to comfort or edify fellow believers.

Many men, however, quite naturally favor the idea of complete silence for women and sound like they enjoy expounding this passage. Listen to William Hendriksen:

Though these words and their parallel in 1 Corinthians 14:33-35 may sound a trifle unfriendly, in reality they are the very opposite. In fact they are expressive of a feeling of tender sympathy and basic understanding. They mean: let a woman not enter a sphere of activity for which by her very creation she is not suited. Let not a bird try to dwell under water. Let not a fish try to dwell on land. Let not a woman yearn to exercise authority over a man by lecturing him in public worship. For the sake both of herself and the spiritual welfare of the church, such unholy tampering with divine authority is forbidden.

In the service of the Word on the day of the Lord a woman should learn, not teach, she should be silent. . . . Moreover this learning in silence should not be with a rebellious attitude of heart, but with complete submissiveness.

Quite apart from his view of women, which we will examine later, and also the fact that Paul does not mention "the day of the Lord," this writer gives a rather horrifying picture of a Christian preacher. Surely the average minister is not "yearning to exercise authority . . . by lecturing" his congregation.

This, and the description of the accredited teacher as "a master to be heard and obeyed" (Hiebert), hardly describes what Christ commissioned his disciples to be and do. He told them to "feed my sheep" and to preach the good news of freedom from sin, of release for the captives and of rescue for the sheep who have gone astray. He gave an invitation—"Come unto me, and I will give you rest"—not a lecture. Granted lectures have their place, but is it at worship and evangelistic services? The tragedy is that early in the history of the church ecclesiastical professionalism silenced not only women but also men, so that today we often hear nothing but a monologue from the minister.

One can well understand that this sometimes seems the only way to have things done "decently and in order," yet we must beware of Christianity developing that "elitism" which characterized the evolution of all the major religions and which was especially apparent in the priestcraft of medieval Christendom, so well described by Robert Brow in his book *Religion*. The outbreak of home Bible studies and body-life emphasis at the present time is no doubt a swing of the pendulum in the opposite direction.

Should Women Never Be Heard in a Mixed Audience?
To return to 1 Timothy 2:11, could the "learning in silence" required by Paul really mean, as some men claim, that there should never be women speakers in a church service, that missionary women should never report on their work to mixed audiences in their home church, that women should not be heads of Sunday school departments, teach classes with both sexes in it or give a testimony to a mixed audience—all of which are done to some extent in many branches of the Christian church at home and abroad today? Hendriksen's description of "the service of the Word on the day of the Lord" seems to deny women any divine sanction for even teaching a Sunday school class of their own sex.

As I studied this passage of Scripture in Japan and before I had heard of the probable meaning of "teach," I was forced to take a serious look at my own work. In the beginning, all my contacts had been with college and high school girls, but gradually other invitations had come. For example, for some years I had, at the invitation of the pastor, been teaching an English Bible class in a Japanese church as an evangelistic outreach. The majority of those attending the class were male university students, mostly non-Christians, although a few from a nearby seminary also came. This was certainly not an "official church service" and I do not think I "lorded it over them." But was Paul saying that I should not be teaching male students anything (even Latin to seminarians?) or only that teaching them the Bible was wrong, even though some of these students would never look at it in any other situation?

Should I be taking my turn, with the rest of the Christian college faculty, as a chapel speaker? At first, I had spoken more in the line of testimony, on Christian journalism or on international communism and its methods of infiltrating Christian groups as I had seen it at the London School of Economics and Political Science in pre-war years and later in China. But there is a limit to that kind of subject.

Looking at that passage, I concluded that Paul might not be happy to see me on that platform. But more important: Was God equally displeased? Availing myself of James' promise, "If any of you lack wisdom, let him ask of God" (1:5), the next time I was asked to speak in chapel I refused, having a good excuse for that date, and prayed that God would guide in whether I would be asked again. The request was repeated soon after, and, without telling him why, I asked my husband if he would like to speak instead of me. "When you are out there anyway, why should I go all that way?" was his response. (A three-hour round trip was involved.) The man who asked me to speak in chapel is now president of one of the outstanding Bible colleges in the States, and the Japanese pastor one of Japan's best evangelists; so all things considered, I felt this was God's assurance that I was doing his will.

Are there other reasons which can legitimately be added to this admittedly subjective ground for what may appear to be the ignoring of a scriptural injunction? One explanation for Paul's statement might be that at Corinth and Ephesus, where Timothy was working when Paul wrote to him, the main deities were the goddesses Venus and Diana. This apparently resulted in most obscene and disorderly "worship." So possibly the women there had little idea of propriety at first, and any participation by women in the Christian services might be misunderstood by outsiders.

It was a time when the majority of pagan women were illiterate, and the few who were not were often of doubtful morals or notorious in other ways. Cara Afrania, for example, a Roman Senator's wife and herself an attorney, was so vehement in her court arguments that the Senate decided to bar all women lawyers from the courtrooms forever! Calvin also mentions this woman as an outstanding example of the lack of "the modesty that becomes a female."

Pythagoras had said, "Three things are greatly to be feared: fire, water, and woman"; and Seneca that "woman and ignorance are the two greatest calamities in the world." Jewish women, as we have seen, had a very inferior place in the synagogue and were not allowed to teach the smallest children, even their own.

With mingled contempt and fear of women prevalent, it seems unlikely that many men would be drawn to Christianity if women were in positions of leadership; and Paul's greatest concern was for the spread of the gospel. We have other instances where he accommodated himself to local conditions in spite of its being against his general principle. Although he had "no small dissension" with Jewish believers who taught that all Christians must be circumcised (Acts 15:1-2), he circumcised Timothy before going on a missionary journey because the Jews of that area knew Timothy's father was Greek (Acts 16:3). Thus, though he believes in principle that there is no longer Jew and Gentile, male and female in Christ, perhaps for the sake of the gospel he is accommodating himself to local thinking.

Commentators' Views Change with Time As I studied all the commentaries in the Tokyo Christian College library, I noted how the remarks differed according to the age in which they were written. This reveals that some of the most learned, orthodox and dedicated interpreters of Scripture are nevertheless strongly influenced by their environment.

One of the early fathers, Chrysostom "the golden

mouthed," succinctly sums the whole matter up by saying, "The woman taught once and ruined all."

Calvin, writing in 1546, in one place upholds the injunction that women should not teach, not so much on the ground of divine edict as of logic and propriety: "Unquestionably, wherever even natural propriety has been maintained, women have in all ages been excluded from the public management of affairs. It is the dictate of common sense that female government is improper and unseemly."

Some of the nineteenth-century commentators express great concern for the temptations women might fall into if they take part in a meeting. One feels that public speaking or asking questions is "calculated to foster woman's vanity," especially if the question is "keen and pert"! Some wax eloquent on woman's susceptibility to guile and persuasion, and P. Fairbairn, writing in Edinburgh in 1874, is almost lyrical in describing some male characteristics and capabilities:

She [woman] lacks, by the very constitution of nature, the qualities necessary for such a task, . . . the equability of temper, the practical shrewdness and discernment, the firm, independent, regulative judgment, which are required to carry the leaders of important interests above first impressions and outward appearances, to resist solicitations, subtle entanglements, and fierce conflicts, to cleave unswervingly to the right.

There must have been some wonderful men in Scotland in 1874!

While agreeing that many men have a superior power of objective and analytical thinking, I cannot help feeling that the above writer forgot for a moment that the human heart, male and female, is "deceitful above all things and desperately wicked." How many men are there in the Bible of whom his description would be accurate? Through patriarchs, judges, kings, prophets and disciples, we see men who made serious errors of judgment. While the situation might have been worse had women held any positions of responsibility, the history of the church has not been conspicuously bright in spite of its all-male leadership. Mary Baker Eddy and a few others apart, from Gnosticism right down to modernism and the heresies of certain well-known bishops, the onus for departing from scriptural truth lies rather heavily on masculine shoulders.

Some more recent commentaries make no attempt to prove the inferiority or innate inability of women, perhaps because a half century and more of coeducation and women's increasing participation in public life have proved that some women, at least, can fulfill responsibilities creditably, and even make excellent teachers.

William Barclay has come a long way from Chrysostom: "This is a passage which cannot be read out of its historical context. It springs entirely from the situation in which it was written. It is written against a double background." He discusses first the Jewish background, which we have already touched on, adding that in Jewish law a woman was not a legal person; she was a thing, entirely at the disposal of her husband or father, forbidden to learn the law, having no part in·the synagogue service. For her even to read the Scripture in that place would be to "lessen the honor of the congregation."

Dealing next with the Greek background, Barclay notes that a respectable Greek woman led a very confined life, living in her own quarters where none but her husband came and not even appearing for meals. He also speaks of the conditions in Greek religions which we have mentioned, maintaining that if a woman had taken an active part the church would inevitably have gained the reputation of

being the resort of loose and immoral women. He concludes,

We must not read this passage as a barrier to all women's work and
service within the church. We must read it in the light of its Jewish
background, and in the light of the situation in a Greek city. And we
must look for Paul's permanent views in the passage which tells us
that the differences are wiped out, and that men and women, slaves
and freemen, Jews and Gentiles are all eligible to serve Christ.

Do Such Views Undermine the Infallibility of Scripture?

Do such views in any way undermine the doctrine of the in-
fallibility of Scripture? We firmly believe the Bible is the
Word of God. We open it and read, "Let the woman learn
in silence with all subjection. But I suffer not a woman to
teach, nor to usurp authority over the man, but to be in
silence." That "I" is God speaking, we may conclude, and
certainly we need to be very sure of our ground before in
any way weakening the force of these words.

Just a few verses before, however, the text says, "Some
. . . concerning faith have made shipwreck, of whom is Hy-
menaeus and Alexander; whom I have delivered unto Satan that they may learn not to blaspheme" (1:19-20). Is that
God speaking, and is this a divine eternal principle for dealing with those who lose their faith? Or is it Paul telling Timothy about something he has done?

Dealing with the theory that the intent of the instructions
for women may be limited to the time in which they were
written, the large majority of commentators, as we have
seen, are quite sure that this is true with regard to the wearing of pearls and veils. Are there other clear scriptural injunctions about which the church in general holds such a
view? Paul ends both letters to the Corinthians and the first
to the Thessalonians with a command to greet one another

with a holy kiss, but as nominal Christians began to enter the church this practice was so abused that it was finally forbidden. Paul also told the Philippians that "at the name of Jesus every knee should bow" (Phil. 2:10). I have been present in churches where some took this as a literal command and genuflected at every mention of the word *Jesus*, yet all the evangelicals I know ignore this. A little further on in 1 Timothy, Paul commands, "Drink no longer water, but use a little wine for thy stomach's sake" (5:23)—a command about which most Bible-believing Christians are silent!

Other instances of Paul's commands which are not usually followed today are "Owe no man anything" (Rom. 13:8), which could conceivably include mortgages and credit cards. Then, "I exhort . . . first of all, supplications, prayers, intercessions and giving of thanks, be made for all men; for kings, and for all that are in authority" (1 Tim. 2:1-2), yet in many fundamental churches it is rare to hear these authorities prayed for. Also, Paul's requirement that overseers and elders must have well-controlled children (1 Tim. 3:4) often seems ignored.

There are, I believe, two further examples of greater importance. The first is Christ's command to his disciples that they should wash one another's feet. This seems very specific, but there is no evidence in the Scriptures that they actually did this. Only the widows put on the church roll seem to have been required to do it (1 Tim. 5:10). Very few churches today practice this, probably because a change in footwear, paved roads and improved transportation have made it unnecessary.

The second concerns the letter on conduct sent to Gentile converts by the council at Jerusalem. After much heated discussion, the participants finally reach a conclusion. James then wrote that it was the considered opinion of all the apostles "and of the Holy Ghost" that Gentile believers did not have to be circumcised but that all should abstain "from meats offered to idols, and from blood, and from things strangled, and from fornication" (Acts 15:29). Leviticus 3:17 is emphatic on one of these points, too: "It shall be a *perpetual* statute for your generations throughout all your dwellings, that ye eat neither fat nor blood." Yet I have never heard of a Bible-believing church which teaches this requirement today. And I know many ministers who relish a rare steak or a roast of beef dripping with bloody juices, although there is no later word in the Scriptures to indicate that these things have been abrogated.

All these examples of omission by the church would not necessarily justify ignoring 1 Timothy 2:11. As the study of hermeneutics indicates, however, and some commentators such as Donald Guthrie have pointed out, "Reserve must be exercised in deducing universal principles from particular cases." Few churches teach and practice baptism for the dead, for instance, although Paul speaks of it with apparent approval (1 Cor. 15:29).

A further possibility is that Paul is referring only to wives. In *Jerusalem in the time of Jesus* Jerimias has a very significant description of a wife. "The wife was obliged to obey her husband as she would a master . . . the husband was called *rab*—indeed this obedience was a religious duty. Like a non-Jewish slave, and a child under age, a woman has over her a man who is her master; and this likewise limits her participation in divine service, which is why, from a religious point of vew, she is inferior to a man."

A famous rabbi once gave his proselyte Gentile slave his freedom, to make the necessary quorum for a synagogue meeting. A woman presumably could never be considered free from bondage to a husband then. Thus Paul probably had married women in mind, and not necessarily all women in his restriction.

Now that in many countries slavery is abolished, and wives are no longer legally "under a master", does this make any difference? This is the question theologians must now decide. Certainly we don't get Paul's words repeated elsewhere in Scripture, and in both Old and New Testaments God raised women to positions of success-ful leadership, as well as in much missionary work in the last century.

Is it possible, then, to reason that Paul was just telling Timothy, "Personally, I don't allow women to teach" (Phillips), and then stating his reasons? He does not claim this is God's permanent command, nor demand that Tim-othy follow his example.

Most English versions of the Bible printed in paragraphs have 1 Timothy 2:8-15 as one paragraph. It is curious that almost all men ignore the injunction to lift up their holy hands in prayer, insist that women *may* wear pearls and look attractive, and largely bypass verse 15 with all its problems about being saved through childbirth; yet they take the intermediate verses, 11-14, at face value as God's basic eter-nal rule. Then they have to wriggle their way around Gala-tians 3:28, the instances of women prophesying and having positions of leadership, and Priscilla teaching Apollos with such beneficial results. They also have to close their eyes to Joel's and Peter's declaration that God promised that in the last days he would pour out his Spirit on sons and daughters and they would prophesy and to the evidence that this did happen at Pentecost.

Of course, the fact that Paul refers back to Adam and Eve in 1 Timothy 2:13-14 does suggest a universal element in the matter. So to evaluate this subject fully we must examine the validity of the reason Paul gives for not letting women teach. We will look at this and related texts dealing with the basic nature of woman in the next two chapters.

12
WOMAN: THE SECOND AND SUBORDINATE SEX?

There were several phrases in the biblical passages we studied in chapters 9—11 with which we did not deal fully. They are ones which many theologians have taken to indicate the basic inferiority and subordination of all women to all men—deriving either from creation itself or else from the Fall—and they are in fact involved in the reasoning behind some of Paul's restrictions. Though some men think these phrases refer only to a wife's relationship to her husband, since the word *woman* is used we must first consider whether these phrases have a more general sense.

What Is the Meaning of Headship?   In 1 Corinthians 11 we read, "The head of the woman is the man. . . . [The man] is the image and glory of God: but the woman is the glory of the man. For the man is not of the woman; but the woman

149

of the man. . . . Nevertheless neither is the man without the woman, neither the woman without the man, in the Lord. For as the woman is of the man, even so is the man also by the woman; but all things of God (vv. 3, 7-8, 11-12).

Many men think the meaning of the first sentence is obvious: Man is the ruler. The Boldreys, think, however, that *Paul was punning on the word "head."* . . . *Rosh the Hebrew word for head is often translated in the Septuagint by* arche *the Greek word which may mean "rule" but just as often means "beginning." In this context Paul speaks of Christ "the* head *of the body, the church: who is the* beginning, *the* firstborn *from the dead" (Col. 1:18). To be the "head" is related to being "first" . . . but priority of time neither necessarily nor universally leads to priority of rank. . . . When Paul spoke of woman's head being the man, he was emphasizing man's temporal priority and woman's derivation from him; this is further substantiated in verse 8.*

Most, however, view man's "headship" as proof that he is boss and the woman his subordinate, and believe that man is to be uncovered in worship to demonstrate the distinction. One writer in the *Pulpit Commentary* tells us that Paul opted for the Greek method of worshiping with uncovered head for men, as opposed to the Jewish wearing of the Tallith, because "the Christian who is in Christ may stand with unveiled face in the presence of the Father." But isn't a woman believer also "in Christ"?

Many commentators like the idea of man being in God's image and having his glory. (Paul mentions only the man in this regard, but Genesis includes the woman.) One man in the *Pulpit Commentary* states, "Man reflects God; woman, in her general nature in this earthly and temporal dispensation, reflects the glory of man." Isn't man's nature also in "this earthly and temporal dispensation"?

When one thinks of the varieties of men's uncovered

heads in the average church today, in what way do they reflect the glory of God? I have sat behind tribesmen who, when they removed their turbans, had heads visibly alive with vermin; others with eyes encrusted with discharge from various diseases. By faith I saw them as sons of God, heirs with Christ, people changed into his likeness; but not merely because they belonged to the male sex and had their heads uncovered.

Woman the Glory of Man   With the exception of James Hurley's recent article, no commentator I have read has attempted to explain how exactly woman is the glory of man, though one suggests "she is as moonlight to his sunlight"—which does not sound very glorious. Usually the commentators are more specific about the part of their own sex; for example, man is the image and glory of God "in face and form" or "in his powers of thought, creativity and ability to rule."

I found no clear explanation for this puzzling thought of Paul's until I encountered Hurley's article. Hurley begins with Paul's hierarchy of God—Christ—man—woman, assumes that the woman is under the authority of her husband and tries to show that her hairstyle demonstrated this fact. With regard to the words that the man is the image and glory of God, and the woman the glory of man, Hurley points out that Paul is not citing Genesis 1:26, which says "image and likeness":

Man in his authority relation to creation and to woman, images the dominion of God over creation (a central theme of the whole of Gen. 1) and the headship of Christ over his church. The woman has a corresponding but different role to play. The woman is not called to image God in the relation which she sustains to her husband; she is rather to show loving obedience.

Then he comes to the term *glory*, which is used both of the man and the woman. Concerning this he says,

Man is relationally the glory of God as he is in appropriate relation to him: under God, thereby pointing to God's dominion, over the remainder of creation, thereby reflecting dominion. In such a relation man is free to be what he truly is, and shows truly what he is meant to be. A woman is the glory of her husband as she stands in a proper relation to him and demonstrates the truth concerning her created role.

In the sense developed above, and within the marriage relationship, the role of image is an active one while that of glory is passive. In this sense therefore the man ought to be designated the image and glory of God, and the woman the glory of man.

As mentioned before, this does present Paul's words as a more unified argument and may be what he was thinking. Whether Hurley's idea of "headship" is really justified by the Genesis account of creation or whether the Boldreys' version is right is hard to determine without a careful study of Genesis. This husband and wife relationship which Hurley suggests is hardly an exact parallel with that of Christ and God. Christ left equality with the Father (Phil. 2:6) to come to this earth as God manifest in the flesh and has returned to reign in heaven as King of Kings and Lord of Lords. It is true that while on earth he submitted to the Father's will, but he also said, "I and the Father are one" and "If ye have seen me, ye have seen the Father." This is hardly the passive role Hurley posits and, in fact, Paul had started out comparing the woman to man relationship as like Christ to God; so it hardly seems justifiable then to make the man image *both* God and Christ.

Subject Because of Eve   A related text is 1 Corinthians 14:34, which the AV inaccurately translates as "but *they are*

commanded to be under obedience, as also saith the law." More correctly the NASV puts "Let the women subject themselves" and the NEB says that the women "should keep their place." The Greek word used here (*hypotasso*) was originally a military term denoting inferior rank, and in the papyri it was used for "appendages" to documents. The Greek voice, however, indicates that this is something the women are requested to do themselves, not something others are to impose on them. Even if the law had said so (which some regard as doubtful, as we shall see later), had not Paul said elsewhere that Christians are no longer under the law?

With regard to 1 Timothy 2:11-14, Hendriksen rejects the view that these directions about women might be based on contemporary conditions, insisting rather that they are based on an eternal principle. This does appear to be Paul's view: "Let the woman learn in silence with all subjection. . . . For Adam was first formed, then Eve. And Adam was not deceived, but the woman being deceived was in the transgression."

Literally this is "has become a transgressor" (Greek perfect expressing an abiding state—Guthrie). One commentator tells us this would better be translated by the English past tense, but, according to W. Lock, Paul's idea was that "the woman 'passed into and has remained in the position of the transgressor.' " And Lock adds, "Possibly a quote from the Jewish oral law, scornful of women, makes the perfect tense more natural."

Not only the rabbinic schools but many theologians after them, as well as most pagan religions, of course, have been firmly convinced of the inferiority of women. In these verses Paul's reasoning is that woman was made after man, from man and for man, and she was deceived by the devil while he was not. So some men have seen two basic principles implied here: first, that woman was created second and therefore subordinate to man; second, that woman is the weaker and more sinful sex. James Strachan tells us,

According to rabbinic casuistry, Adam was created first and sinned second, Eve was created second and sinned first. Therefore let woman recognize that she is both weaker and worse than man, and let her never attempt either to teach or control him! The premise of this argument—in which the rabbis to their shame delighted—finds no confirmation either in science or experience.

If true, this last statement is certainly encouraging for women. But of primary importance, before the findings of science or experience, is whether there is ground for such a view in the Scriptures. It is interesting that J. B. Phillips, who spent much time studying the New Testament documents to make his paraphrase in modern English, also sees these views of Paul as having a rabbinic source, while at the same time coming to believe the Scriptures to be divinely inspired:

It was not until I realized afresh what the man [Paul] had actually achieved, and suffered, that I began to see that here was someone who was writing . . . by the inspiration of God himself. Sometimes you can see the conflicts between the pharisaic spirit of the former Saul (who could write such grudging things about marriage and insist on the perennial submission of women) and the Spirit of God who inspired Paul to write that in Christ there is neither Jew nor Greek . . . male nor female.

What Is Woman? In Scripture God did create two sexes, however, and obviously with some purpose. So we shall now try to discover what a female really is—primarily from Scripture, but with a brief glance at science and experience to see whether Strachan's statement is justified. We must go further back than the New Testament and scientists' and theologians' opinions to find what woman is. Is she a female human being, a part of humanity who happens to have certain biological and psychological differences from the male? Or is she an entirely separate and secondary species made just for the need of man? The answer to this important question is in the scriptural account of creation.

Our problem in understanding the Genesis account fully is that the Hebrew word for mankind is the same as that later made into a personal name for the first male, Adam. So we cannot always tell which meaning is intended; translators vary, some rendering "Adam," some "man." Genesis 1:26-31 says:

God said, Let us make man[kind] in our image, after our likeness, and let them have dominion over the fish of the sea, and over the fowl of the air, and over the cattle, and over all the earth. . . . So God created man[kind] in his own image . . . ; male *and* female *created he them. And God blessed* them, *and God said unto* them, *Be fruitful and multiply . . . and* subdue it *[the earth]: and have* dominion. . . . *God saw everything that he had made, and, behold, it was very good.*

We have a summary of this again in Genesis 5:1-2, and here modern versions bring out the meaning more clearly: "In the day when God created man, he made him in the likeness of God. He created them male and female, and he blessed them and named them Man[kind] in the day when they were created" (NASB). The New Berkeley Version has "He created them male and female. He blessed them and called them human at the time of their creation."

From these passages it seems clear that God created humanity, male and female, in his image, and gave them both dominion over the earth. Many theologians and rabbis ignore these, however, and look only at Genesis 2 where we find a more detailed account of the creation of man first and then woman. There we are told God formed man of the dust and then "breathed into his nostrils the breath of lives [plural in Hebrew]; and man became a living soul [being]" (v. 7).

After an unspecified period of time but still within "the sixth day" evidently, "God said, It is not good that man should be alone; I will make him an help meet for [lit: *corresponding to*] him" (v. 18). The animals were next brought before the man and he gave them names, "but for Adam there was not found an help meet for him" (v. 20). So God caused a deep, anesthetizing sleep to come over him. For some unexplained reason (possibly Jewish tradition) most English translations state that God took one of the man's "ribs," but according to Archdeacon Wilberforce this same word occurs forty-two times in the Old Testament, and is nowhere else translated "rib," but "side," "sides," "corners" or "chambers."

From whatever was taken from the man God made a woman, and brought her to Adam. McNally suggests that in great excitement he exclaimed something like: "At last! This is me!" Not another animal, but "bone of my bone and flesh of my flesh!" There is no suggestion woman was weaker physically or inferior because she appeared last. She could have been the crowning glory of creation since not until after her appearance does it say, "God saw everything that he had made, and, behold, it was very good" (Gen. 1:31). It is possible he delayed the formation of the woman so that the man would really experience a need for her and appreciate her the more when God gave her to him, rather than that she was a mere appendage or afterthought.

After the woman's formation the Bible continues, "Therefore, shall a man leave his father and his mother, and shall cleave unto his wife: and they shall be one flesh" (Gen. 2:24). They originated from one flesh, were separated into male and female, and in the divine provision of marriage would again become one flesh. There is nothing about the man ruling over the woman, only that he leave his parents and cleave to his wife; together they would form a new independent unit.

This divine pattern has rarely been followed in pagan societies, or even Jewish and Christian in some areas. Rather, the wife is taken into the husband's home to be ruled by the mother-in-law and other males in the family. Lange expresses the superiority of God's plan thus:

With a stroke of the pen, the Biblical view of the world places itself above the aboriginal doctrines of every heathen people, and all national pride. . . . In a few lines it records the equality by birth of the male and female sexes, the mystical nature of true marriage, the sanctity of the married and domestic life, and condemns the heathen degradation of woman, sexual lawlessness, and also the theosophic and monkish contempt of sexual nature.

What Is Woman? Biologically All are aware of the anatomical differences in the normal male and female body. But that they are not separate species is evident from the fact that some are born with a mixture, such as internal female organs but a penis and empty scrotum outside. Or what appears like a penis may prove to be an enlarged clitoris and the scrotum fused labia. That these are not so rare as some suppose is indicated in the rabbinic teaching that "one of doubtful sex" and "one of double sex" were included with women, slaves, children, deaf-mutes and so forth, and thus not required to go to the temple for the three great feasts.

We are not told in Genesis how God dealt with the part

he took from the man to form the woman, nor are we sure of what it consisted. Could part of it have been the X chromosome? Of the 46 chromosomes in the human body only two vary according to sex, although 23 are contributed by each parent. The female normally has two X chromosomes, the male an X and a Y. Some male criminals of low mentality and strong aggressive traits examined in prisons recently have been found to have two Y chromosomes, but there is no firm proof yet that chromosomes determine masculine or feminine traits.

Traditionally, society has tended to stereotype male and female, whereas modern genetical research recognizes a great range of types neither clearly male or female. From this Margaret Evening concludes that biological sexuality is not a major factor for "a new creature in Christ." "All human beings are a combination of both sexes and wholeness implies the accepting of one's femininity (the Anima) as a man, and one's masculinity (the Animus) as a woman."

Bernard Ramm, on the other hand, states that every cell in the body is coded masculine or feminine at conception. "If to be a woman or to be a man is a *total way* of existing, then the categories of 'superior' and 'inferior' are secondary. The issue then is that man lives his life in a *masculine* way, and the woman lives her life in a *feminine* way. The real issue is what is the Biblical doctrine of the feminine role, and what the Biblical doctrine of the masculine role?"

It would still seem possible to say that the masculine "way of existing" has been far superior to the feminine in many cultures! Apart from the husband-wife relationship, how do we live in a masculine and feminine way? The average day of a man and a woman high school teacher or doctor in the West would be lived very similarly, though granted their view of, and reaction to, their respective students or patients might differ a little; and he might shave his face and she her legs. On the whole, however, these two would live much more similarly than the male doctor and a man from a primitive tribe of Irian Jaya. About the only thing the doctor would have in common with that man would be the power to impregnate.

Many today fear to indicate superiority or inferiority in relation to sex, and instead put the emphasis on "role." Actually this is neither a scriptural term nor a scientific one. While it sounds like a nice theory, useful in the problems of family, business and church relationships, doubt is now cast by some psychologists on its universal application to all men and all women. Not all agree, of course. Clyde Narramore claims, "When God created a companion for the first man in the garden of Eden he endowed her with the attributes of beauty, gentleness, love, a sensitive nature, and an understanding heart. These have become symbols of womanhood. They form the framework for development of every little girl." Nowhere does the Bible contain this prescription for girls, however, nor are any of these characteristics actually attributed to Eve.

While many have thought that male and female characteristics are inherent in the coded cells of the fetus, the theory is now advanced that they are conditioned by cultural upbringing. John Money, member of the National Institute of Mental Health's Task Force on Homosexuality, holds that there are only four imperative differences between the sexes: Women menstruate, gestate and lactate; men impregnate. These are basic powers or functions which cannot be interchanged (and will certainly affect action to some extent). Role is a much more elastic term, its connotation for the sexes being apt to change considerably in different ages and cultures.

Money's view is based on numerous observations and experiments. In addition to hermaphrodites, he cites the case of a family with identical twin boy babies. When these were circumcised, the penis of one was burned off by a surge of electrical current in the cauterizing needle. The parents were advised to bring this baby up as a girl, with the help of plastic surgery. Nine years later "she" seems psychologically to be a girl and behaves very differently from the identical twin brother. Such instances are creating doubt in some scientists' minds that major sexual psychological differences are immutably set by the genes at conception.

No one is yet sure what causes a fetus to be male or female, many conjecturing that it is determined by the time in the menstrual cycle at which conception takes place. Others suggest environmental stress is the factor. The father's sperm determines the sex, and if seven weeks before conception the Y-bearing sperms are damaged, the resulting fetus will be female. Statistics at Bristol University are even pointing to such things as prolonged smog, or sudden deluges temporarily softening drinking water, as being connected with sudden regional increases in female births.

From experiments conducted on animals, Money believes that in the normal process of sex differentiation, if the genes order the production of the hormone androgen the embryo becomes a male; otherwise it becomes a female. One interesting finding is that androgen not only shapes the external organs, but also "programs" parts of the brain, so that some types of behavior may come more naturally to one sex than the other. For instance, both males and females can "mother" children—the necessary circuits are there in the brain—but the "threshold" for releasing this behavior is higher in males than females. This is certainly an interesting conclusion from experiments with animals.

We also hear sometimes of human widowers who successfully "mother" their children; and many more widows, as well as wives of military men, who of necessity have had to take over "the managing of affairs" for varying lengths of time, and with some success. The two world wars also saw women undertaking almost all types of work on the home front, as well as many serving with the military forces.

What Is Woman? In Experience   After the first four years of life, Money thinks, there is little hope of breaking down the sex-role stereotypes which will usually have been established by parents and friends by then. But from war experiences noted above and my own school days (very different from America), I doubt this is so. In England then co-education was rare, so in my schools teachers and students were all female. Most of us were unaware the male was "the head." I hardly knew any males, having no brothers, no church young people's group. Females far outnumbered males in Europe then, and our education and training were not for the purpose of competing with men, but to prepare us for an interesting, useful life of benefit to community and country and at the same time ensuring economic security.

Maybe the "threshold" was higher for us, but we managed to have presidents of clubs, captains of sports teams, and so on. One girl I sat next to in high school was elected a member of Parliament, and a few years ago was made a life peer for her contribution to the country in the industrial relations field. Three of my class of thirty-five became doctors. The one who took me to the meeting where I found Christ has "manned" a clinic in an isolated area of India for many years, with only one nurse to help her. Another had the rare distinction of winning a math scholarship to Oxford University where there were few women in those days.

The publication marking the school's 80th anniversary records many interesting occupations. One of our earliest alumni was Dr. Edith Brown, founder of the famed Ludhiana Christian Medical College and hospital in India. One girl, a year my senior, is an architect who has worked in England, West Africa, Arabia and now India. Many are working in different parts of the world, some as missionaries, I am glad to say. Another is a lawyer, one a national broadcaster, one Principal of the Goodhousekeeping Institute which entails a wide national ministry. Others are journalists, agricultural specialists, as well as the more ordinary social workers, probation officers, teachers at all levels of education, nurses, doctors, secretaries, wives and mothers.

I realize now that we had a very fine, highly qualified and dedicated faculty who, though all were unmarried, must have felt they had some useful purpose in life. May I stress again that there was no idea of "competing with men," for no men teachers would have thought of teaching in girls' schools.

It was the same when I began my career as medical social worker in a Christian hospital for women and children in the slums of London. (Many women in those days were too embarrassed to go to a man doctor, partly because it was the Depression and they had no decent clothing, and the only free treatment was at the big teaching hospitals where there was always a group of observing male students present.) The two doctors, former missionaries, who started this little hospital were women, as were the visiting specialists and dentist, and also pharmacist and nurses. I began my Christian ministry to adults by taking my turn giving short evangelistic messages in this hospital's out-patient waiting room, and taking devotions in the wards. Our head was not a man, but Christ.

To summarize what a woman is, then, we find from Scripture that she is a human being made by God in his image, of the same bone and flesh as man, a counterpart for him, and together they are to have dominion over the earth. From science, observation and experience we further know there are three biological functions possible only to woman, and which determine some of her "roles" at certain times and circumstances; but at least some of her characteristics and roles may be the result of upbringing and training rather than inherent biological necessities. In any case, it appears that "roles" are not so much genetically determined as some theologians claim. And, therefore, there is a strong possibility that when Paul spoke of the headship of the man he was referring only to the marriage relationship.

Is Woman Subordinate Because Second?   Most theologians and many others are quite happy with the rabbinic teaching that because Adam was formed first he was therefore naturally superior to Eve. As McNally points out, we do not know if the first human was solely male or hermaphrodite. But even if he were all male, creation was in ascending order, from creeping things, to animals, to man, to woman.

God created woman because man was incomplete or in a "not good" state without her. Paul Tournier in *To Understand Each Other* says that it is a mysterious fact that no one comes to know himself through introspection or in the solitude of his personal diary but only in his meeting with other persons. "That is why in the beginning of the Bible God

163

says it is not good that the man should be alone. Man here means human being: It is not good that the human being should be alone." A human being needs fellowship; he needs a partner, a real encounter with another. He needs to understand others and to sense that others understand him.

Tournier claims, "Such is the very intention of God in instituting marriage, according to the Bible. Alone, a man marks time and becomes very set in his ways. In the demanding confrontation which marriage constitutes, he must ever go beyond himself, develop, grow up into maturity."

Many of the early commentators would regard this as heresy, for most believed Paul taught that since woman was created "of and for man" then the priority of man's creation places him in a position of superiority. Because she has been made as a "help" for him, that obviously means she is to be a kind of servant, someone to wait on him and someone for him to ejaculate into, as Muslims and many others have believed. "The woman is expressly the man's 'helper' which underlies her inferior position." She is certainly not meant to constitute a "demanding confrontation" to help the male to maturity!

Actually this Hebrew word *ezer* (help, succour) used of Eve in Genesis 2:18 is often used to describe God himself, the "helper" of his people. (See Ex. 18:4; Deut. 33:7; Ps. 27:9 and many other passages.) "It indicates one who comes to another's aid, ... and occurs in the Bible sixteen times of a superior, five times of an equal, but never of an inferior. Adam needed someone like himself; Eve, derived from his very being, supplied that need as his equal, as himself. This is a practice of oneness, not of subordination," the Boldreys tell us.

How different this view is from Calvin's: "The reason women are prevented from teaching is that it is not compatible with their status, which is to be subject to men, whereas to teach implies superior authority and status." It would be "a mingling of earth and heaven" for women to teach. He admits that even men teachers are subject to kings and magistrates, but says there is no absurdity in man's commanding and obeying at the same time in different relationships. This does not apply to women, however, "who by nature are born to obey." Calvin considered that this was the law God imposed on them from the beginning: "The teaching of Moses is that woman was created later, to be a kind of appendage to the man, on the express condition that she should be ready to obey him." Calvin not only held that this subordination was innate in woman's creation but also that God inflicted it upon woman by way of punishment. He sees this as rather a contradiction; but it must mean the subjection was less agreeable after the fall, he concludes. (I will deal with the latter in the next chapter.)

Even Clyde Narramore, who has wide experience and has given helpful counsel to thousands, after a good chapter on the unmarried woman says in *A Woman's World*, "Woman was not made for herself, but to complete the man." Is the implication that man *is* made for himself? Are not each made for God? Otherwise a single woman must constantly have the frustrating feeling that somewhere there is her Mr. Right whom she somehow cannot locate or else that she was born useless, with no purpose in life.

Hendriksen, in the quotation given earlier, also seems to have the idea that woman is a somewhat subhuman sort of creature when he likens her to a bird trying to swim under water or a fish trying to live on land. Why not use another human as an illustration, for example, a woman's trying to preach or teach is as contrary to her nature as a man's trying to breastfeed a baby? But no, he likens women to something near the bottom of the creaturely scale.

It was a revelation and shock, at first, to read some theologians' views of women (the worst have been subject to editorial cutting), and I wondered if they wrote them thinking only other men would read them. Certainly I had never heard such things in sermons. I have found Paul Tournier's book, referred to earlier in the chapter, helpful in understanding some of the differences between men and women, however. He says men usually think in general theoretical terms, unrelated to people. They may expound magnificent theories, such as how the world should be governed or how to achieve universal peace, a pollution-free environment and so on, while if one of their wives were present she would probably say, "What about carrying out the garbage or taking an interest in your son's learning difficulties?" So probably most of these commentators had no real women in mind as they were expounding these passages. I, on reading them, immediately think of missionary women I have heard who are excellent speakers and of some men I know who would feel uncomfortable in the pulpit or before a Sunday school class.

In the introduction to the Bible study *Learning to Be a Woman*, K. G. Smith says some rather strange things. "Woman can only be called virtuous [in the sense of Prov. 31] when she has come to understand . . . her role in life as God intended. . . . Woman as God designed her can only be understood and appreciated as she is viewed in her position beside man." Then the author states frankly that his "entire study has been cast as it were in the framework of a man's point of view. After all, that's where a woman lives her life."

I suppose because until very recently women have been

in the minority in North America and therefore most have
been married, men there have no conception of how such
statements can affect a single girl who with no man beside
her may be running an orphanage, a girls' school or a home
for the blind in a foreign country or even having the responsibility of a widowed mother at home. It seems cruel
and untrue to say that all the Christian women doctors, dentist and nurses at the little hospital I worked at in the slums
of London could not be understood or appreciated, that
they did not have "the secret of a woman's understanding
herself" and even could not be "called virtuous," just because they did not live beside a man.

Certainly sex can be a beautiful experience. God himself
planned it in love for his creation. But he did have a few
other things in mind for his people to do. As we saw in the
study of the Gospels, Christ rebuked the bystanders for
evaluating his mother merely in terms of womb and breasts,
and he did not tell Martha and Mary they ought to be married to be able to understand themselves. Paul actually said
it was better not to marry, but devote oneself without distraction to serving the Lord.

Gladys Hunt's *Ms. Means Myself* has a good description
of the spiritually liberated woman who has had a personal
encounter with God:

*If you were to ask her, "Are you most conscious of being a person or
a woman?" she would affirm her personhood. Healthy women are
conscious of being persons, as men are. They are persons who are
women, not women trying to find personhood. It seems accurate to
say that men make women most conscious of their womanhood, and
I suppose the reverse is true as well. But an unhealthy woman is
one who has no sense of self except as she exists in the eyes of men.*

How true that is! I heard recently of a senior in high
school who wasted and worried away her whole final year

fearing she would not get a date for the graduation Prom. Sure enough, she didn't.

It has been a blessing for me to be acquainted with many men of spiritual, intellectual and administrative greatness, through membership in two large interdenominational missions, fellowship with Inter-Varsity Christian Fellowship in several countries and visits to many Christian conferences and well-known churches. God is obviously equipping and using these men for their varied work. But in some of these places one could also meet some women of higher caliber than some men. Why the rabbis should regard all men as automatically superior to all women just because Adam was created before Eve is hard to understand. Perhaps they took too seriously the law of primogeniture, sacrosanct in many countries but which God many times ignored, choosing Jacob above Esau, Joseph above his eleven brothers. Moses, Gideon, David, Solomon—none of them was the oldest in his family.

The Jewish people actually owed their existence to a few women God chose to use. Sarah was responsible for them in the beginning. They were not descended from Abraham's firstborn, and he had children by Keturah after Sarah's death. In Egypt it was the midwives who first thwarted Pharaoh's plan to exterminate the Hebrews; and then Moses' mother and sister with great courage and ingenuity saved his life so that he was able later to lead the people to freedom. Deborah and Jael delivered them from the mighty oppression of Jabin. Through Huldah God chose to reveal his will to King Josiah and the high priest, thus bringing about what was probably the greatest spiritual revival in the history of the Jews. Esther with great bravery and initiative saved the whole Jewish nation from extinction.

So we may conclude that priority of birth, or even creation, does not automatically and necessarily mean superiority in any other way. *The International Standard Bible Encyclopaedia* has some surprisingly strong words on this subject: *Man's historic treatment of woman, due to his conceit, ignorance or moral perversion, has taken her inferiority for granted, and has thus necessitated it by her enslavement and degradation. . . . Her inferiority, subjection and servitude . . . are the severest possible arraignment of man's intelligence and virtue. Natural prudence should have discovered the necessity of a cultured and noble motherhood in order to produce a fine grade of manhood.*

As we have seen, God has not always chosen to promote the firstborn to positions of great responsibility, nor has he always chosen to keep women in positions of subordination. It may also be well to remember that Christ promised that many who are first in this life will be last in the life eternal, and many of the last here will be first there (Mt. 19:30).

13
WOMAN: THE WEAKER AND MORE SINFUL SEX?

In addition to his view that the woman was made on the express condition that she be ready to obey the man, Calvin also felt that since she had seduced the man from God's commandment it was fitting that she should be deprived of all her freedom and placed "under his yoke." He admits that it could reduce women to despair to hear that the whole ruin of the human race was imputed to them, "for what will be the judgment of God upon them!" But Paul seeks to comfort them (in 1 Tim. 2:13-15), and make their condition bearable by reminding them that although they are suffering temporal punishment, the hope of salvation remains to them, Calvin declared. Paul, however, in Romans 5: 12-14 designated Adam as the cause of sin's entering the world.

Fairbairn had much the same view, although he seemed

to see the Fall as Eve's stepping out of her subordinate place and Adam's listening to her, rather than their eating the fruit God had forbidden:

Adam was first formed, then Eve. Thus did God give clear testimony to the headship of man . . . [to his right to stand under the law only to God] while the woman, being formed for him, stands under the law to her husband. And simply by inverting this relative position and calling–the helpmate assuming the place of the head and guide–was the happy constitution of paradise overthrown, and everything involved in disorder and evil. For this sorrowful violation of the primeval order with its disastrous results, the apostle fetches his second reason for fixing . . . the social position of women. "And Adam was not deceived, but the woman being altogether deceived fell," . . . a grand though mournful example, at the commencement of the world's history, of the evil sure to arise if in the general management of affairs woman should quit her proper position as the handmaid of man.

We saw in the last chapter that the Genesis account of creation gives no indication at all of the woman's being placed "under the law to her husband." The suggestion that her sin as the result of being deceived was worse than her husband's seems at first a strange argument to us, since we are inclined to think of sin done in ignorance as less culpable, even if not so regarded legally. In fact Paul himself, in 1 Timothy 1:13, states that he had been a blasphemer and persecutor, "but I obtained mercy because I did it ignorantly in unbelief." In other words he had been deceived by the devil, or his Jewish leaders, as to what Christianity was and had fought against Christ and murdered his followers. It is hard to see how Eve's succumbing to the reasoning of the father of lies was really worse, except perhaps that she was doing it from a state of perfection while Saul of Tarsus was a member of a fallen world.

Is Woman the Weaker Sex?   In his commentary on the Pastoral Epistles Donald Guthrie sees this point, saying, "The serpent deceived the woman, the woman did not deceive the man but persuaded him. Logically this should have made Adam more culpable, but Paul is concerned primarily with the inadvisability of women teachers, and he may have had in mind the greater aptitude of the weaker sex to be led astray."

This idea of women being more easily led astray is a favorite theme with many commentators. It is usually stated as a fact without proof, Eve's action being taken as typical of all womankind. It does not seem to be universally true in experience, however. In a recent Gallup Poll in Canada, for example, people were asked, "Do you believe that religion can answer all or most of today's problems—or is it largely old-fashioned and out of date?" In reply forty percent of the women questioned believed that it can answer most problems while only twenty-eight percent of the men thought so. Which group appears to have been most led astray? (Of course, *religion* is a very wide term, but in Canada the majority of people would still think of it as denoting Christianity.) Again, as has been mentioned already, by far the greater number of Christian heresies have been introduced and supported by men.

Then if Adam sinned with his eyes open, so to speak, just how was he better than Eve? Some have proposed that he only agreed to her suggestion out of a feeling of noble loyalty, determined to "cleave" to her whether in heaven or hell. It would be interesting to know what would have happened to the human race if only Eve had eaten the fruit, but it is profitless to speculate.

Included in the idea of woman's inferiority in the minds of many rabbis, theologians and the majority of mankind is that mentally and morally she is the weaker sex. Her "very creation" makes her unsuitable for teaching, according to Hendriksen, and the ancient rabbis used that as the reason for not teaching her the Torah. Paul does not state this specifically, but it is possible he implies it. One of the commentators in the *Pulpit Commentary* says, "This facility of deception on her part seems to suggest to the apostle her inferiority to men in strength of intellect, and the consequent wrongness of allowing to women an intellectual supremacy over men." Another presumes it is "the *ideal* woman and *ideal* man" which are meant. "It is because the man is supposed to have more brain and soul than the woman that he is the master." But he adds that he knows "not a few cases where the woman is greater in intellect, heart, and all moral goodness" than the husband.

Even if it were true that all women are a little weaker in intellectual capacity than all men, should that necessarily exclude them from taking part in any Christian ministry? In 1 Corinthians Paul tells his readers, "I came with no superiority of eloquence or of wisdom when I announced to you God's revealed truth. . . . My message and my preaching were not in persuasive, learned oratory, but rather in evidence of the Spirit and power, so that your faith might not rest on human wisdom but on divine strength" (1 Cor. 2:1, 4-5, Berkeley). So if God poured out his Spirit on his daughters and handmaidens wouldn't the results be the same? Great human intellect is not essential.

Further, Paul has said in 1:27-29, "God hath chosen the foolish things of the world to confound the wise; and God hath chosen the weak things of the world to confound the things which are mighty . . . and things which are despised, hath God chosen, yea, and things which are not, to bring to nought things that are: that no flesh should glory in his presence." What has been considered more foolish, weak, despised and unmentionable throughout the ages than woman? Therefore it is possible that God could be consistent with his character and intentions by calling and using women in the service of the gospel.

Another man, however, thinks that the "primeval order" —that woman was made for man—governs all her relationships, not only in the family and the church but also in the state. Someone else believes that "the way woman was worked upon by the tempter was emblematic of a natural disposition which unfits her for taking a public position."

As for woman's supposed inability in "the management of affairs" and her facility in being swayed by others, there have been countless cases which have disproved this as universally true, just as there have been a number of men who have had these two failings. Two examples of female competence must suffice here.

The first is a woman mayor in London, Ontario. According to one reporter's account,

since she assumed the mayor's chair, London's city council has experienced a refreshing decline in bickering, meddling, and time wasting. Backslapping has all but vanished. . . . Chunks of parkland have been saved from developers. "Nonestablishment" community groups have been astonished when the mayor came to convince them they had open access to city hall. Businessmen and developers have come to have a grudging respect for Jane's competence.

She also bicycles to work, or hitches a ride with the fire chief rather than piling up a big expense account.

I certainly don't believe men have the monopoly on bickering, meddling and time wasting; if all the council had been women, conditions might not have been better! In addition to this woman's competence, perhaps the presence of both sexes brought out the best in each. Surely God made us complementary not only for the sex act but for many other situations as well. Tournier says, "It is from woman, and under her influence, that man can acquire a feeling for persons. Civilization built by man alone would remain abstract, cold, technical and dehumanized."

Even more astonishing is the effect that the first woman medical student in the English-speaking world, Elizabeth Blackwell, had on her fellow students and professors at Geneva Medical College, New York. From D. C. Wilson's biography, *Lone Woman*, we learn that she felt God calling her to this work but met with every kind of difficulty as she pursued it. Every medical college kept its doors firmly closed against the intrusion of women. Finally the Geneva administration let the students vote, saying if even one was negative they would not admit her. Treating it as a hilarious joke, the students voted unanimously for this unknown monstrosity. The effect of her attending was that they began to behave like gentlemen in class, instead of drowning out the professors with uproar and dirty jokes, as had been the custom particularly in anatomy classes.

Elizabeth felt a divine command to alleviate suffering among women, and she took each step of her preparation with prayer. Even those she intended to help, however, usually spoke evil of her, imagining her to be like a notorious female abortionist in New York at that time. She had the greatest difficulty renting a room from scandalized landladies, and even women from the slums of New York's Ward Eleven, with a population of 54,000 and no medical facilities whatever, were slow in coming to her free clinic.

She eventually founded the New York Infirmary, providing the first possibility for women to intern in the United States and for nurses to train. Some of her unusual practices were to bathe patients, keep careful records and insist on the patient's name and doctor's signature being put on prescriptions. Elizabeth even had the then ridiculous idea that a surgeon should wash his hands and instruments before operating and that each patient should be put on a fresh sheet. The usual practice for a surgeon when operating was to wear his oldest frock coat which gradually became so full of dried blood and puss, it would stand up by itself.

Elizabeth Blackwell also helped found the first women's medical college in her native England. There her friend Florence Nightingale, only through the unhappy circumstances of war, was finally able to introduce the idea of women nurses and "revolutionize the whole health program of the British army." Florence's ideas were later incorporated into the military forces of many countries, including those of the north in the American Civil War, and have probably saved hundreds of thousands of lives since. How many men who experienced hospital care or the benefits of preventive medicine in the many battlefields of the world during this time honestly believe it would have been better to die rather than to have women think up such ideas or leave their "God-appointed place in the home" to become nurses?

It appears, then, that not all women are inferior in intellectual or administrative ability, nor are all easily swayed from a right purpose.

Is Woman More Sinful? When Paul used that perfect tense to describe Eve as becoming and continuing a transgressor, did he mean all that the rabbis implied about woman? It is hard to tell, but let us examine what Genesis states about the Fall. Satan, "the wiliest of all the field animals" and evidently bent on spoiling God's creation, came with subtle lies and half-truths to tempt Eve to disobey God's order. She evidently believed him and was tempted to try the fruit on three counts: It was good for the body, the eyes and the mind. These are the basis for most temptations, it seems, for both men and women; but Eve was certainly the first to take the fruit. Whether she actually ate it first is not absolutely clear but sounds probable. The Berkeley Version has "she took of the fruit and ate; she also gave to her husband, who ate with her. Then the eyes of both were opened" (Gen. 3:6-7). Was Adam alongside all the time, and could he have stopped her? We do not know.

The majority assert that God's later edict was Eve's punishment—that in pain and sorrow (although literally it is "labor," exactly the same word as is used later of the man) she would have many pregnancies and that "thy desire shall be to thy husband, and he shall rule over thee" (Gen. 3:16). Many have said that this means she would have an "inordinate sexual desire for a husband bordering on disease"! A few, however, have suggested that the latter part of God's words to Eve is "descriptive rather than prescriptive," that is, that God was explaining what would be the historical result of being the fallen wife of a fallen man. The Jerusalem Bible has "He will lord it over you," not something God usually approves of. "This was not a new enactment, but a prophecy of the treatment that should come to her," says H. A. Thompson.

In her thesis Jane McNally has an interesting quotation on the word translated "desire":

Drs. Bushnell and Starr follow the Septuagint, Peshitta, Samaritan Pentateuch, Old Latin, Sahidic, Bohairic and Aethiopic Versions in rendering the Hebrew word not "desire" but "turning." In the sixteenth century an Italian Dominican monk, named Pagnino, published his translation of the Hebrew Bible. Influenced by the teaching of the Talmud—the bane of the Jewish race—he rendered the word "lust" or sensual desire. The offensiveness of this rendering becomes apparent when we apply it to Genesis 4:7 where God says to Cain, "Unto thee shall be his desire, and thou shalt rule over him" . . . In the word itself there is no suggestion of libidinousness. . . . It seems to the author that Dr. Bushnell's rendering, "Thou art turning away (from God) to thy husband, and he will rule over thee," is well supported.

The Boldreys also hold this view and believe that Eve usurped *God's* authority, not Adam's, by suggesting he eat the fruit.

Perhaps it is because the Bible mentions that after the Fall Adam and Eve discovered they were naked that lustful sex has been associated with the Fall. As we have already seen, the oral law thought of the Fall as originating in intercourse between the serpent and Eve, and taught that the poison she thus derived was then transmitted to the rest of the human race. Some rabbis later amended this theory, saying the poison was removed from Israel by obedience to the law but remained with the Gentiles. Early church fathers, too, particularly Augustine, continued some of this idea that sex is evil.

Even in 1972, the religion columnist of a Canadian newspaper, writing on the subject of the ordination of women, reported that the Anglican Bishop of Dorchester "naively" said, "Women, unlike men, radiate sex, and their temperament is inappropriate in church. . . . Their ordination would introduce distractions and earthiness into worship." This view, according to the columnist, is based on "the arguments of Scripture and theology rather than sociology and psychology"! It may be the argument of some theologians, but I find no Bible verse expressing such an idea.

Most of us women really do go to church to worship God and learn more about him. There more than in any other place we probably think of ourselves less as women and more as human beings saved by Christ's loving sacrifice. One of the preachers I am privileged to hear frequently is my husband; but I do not ever remember my thoughts being turned to sex while listening to his sermons which are usually interesting and helpful; and certainly not while listening to any other preacher, good, bad or indifferent.

That statement by the bishop reminds me of something a wife said to Charles Shedd: "It seems that all my husband ever thinks about is sex. He interprets every move I make as a mating move. Do *all* men figure *all* of life by sex symbols *all* the time?" Shedd then made a wise observation:

When you examine this sort of thing carefully, you observe an important fact. Man's seeming obsession with sex does not prove that it means more to the male than the female. On the contrary, it may mean the opposite. His sex drive is more of a surface, physical thing. Yours is likely to be much deeper, a matter of spirit and soul. He is more easily aroused. Your stirrings come from farther away inside yourself.

This is how God made us, male and female, and yet how few of us really understand the differences between us and the opposite sex and act in the most helpful way to the other. I am told on good authority that even while preaching men may be sexually aroused; that is the way they are made, and women would be more restrained in dress and action if they realized this. On the other hand, it hardly seems fair for the bishop to impute *his* reactions to the women, label their temperament "inappropriate in church" and claim that the ordination of women would introduce "earthiness into worship." That is already there in his mind and makeup.

One cannot help wondering why the church has not advocated completely separate worship services for men and women if women are so distracting. But since they have been content to have two-thirds of the congregation female, in spite of the disturbing effect, surely just one (probably middle-aged) female in the pulpit would not be really disastrous. She could be robed or dark-suited, like Margaret Heckler who "conducted her first primary campaign in Massachusetts wearing a grey flannel suit at every appearance. It was designed to allow her to blend into the grey male political arena, so voters would be forced to forget she was a woman." While in training for the China Inland Mission we women candidates had to wear staid uniforms calculated to see us safely through the worst areas of London in our evangelistic endeavors. Seeing me in it, my fiancé would sometimes teasingly say he was tempted to break our engagement!

We will look at one more "Christian" view of woman, that of Tertullian, whom W. S. McBirnie calls "the first great genius, after the Apostles, among Christian writers." He certainly had a gift for making his meaning unmistakably clear! He thought women should "dress in humble garb, walking about as Eve, mourning and repentant . . . that she might more fully expiate that which she derives from Eve—the ignominy and odium of human perdition." Addressing women in *De Cultu Feminarum* he says,

Do you not know that you are each an Eve? The sentence of God on this sex of yours lives in this age: the guilt must of necessity live too. You are the devil's gateway: you are the unsealer of that tree: you are the first deserter of the divine law: you are she who persuaded him whom the devil was not valiant enough to attack: you destroyed so easily God's image, man. On account of your desert—that is death—even the Son of God had to die.

I find no Scripture saying that God will judge me for sins

committed by others before my life began or that women are the sole cause of evil in the world. But, thank God, Christ did die for us women as well as for all men who will receive him. Since the church is usually composed of a majority of women and since prisons are very sparsely inhabited by them (thirty men to one woman in England last year, while in North America just over ten percent of the inmates are female), does this mean that woman has to some extent learned her lesson or availed herself of God's provision more readily than man? Admittedly, though, there may be many things displeasing to God which do not rate a prison sentence.

Paul Tournier has some interesting observations about the greater proportion of women in the church:

In the whole area of sex, as in many others, . . . women are in a general and overall sense, more upright than men. Or, at the least, the man is in general more conscious of his sins than the woman is of hers. He is very conscious of his sexual lust, of his lying to his wife or to his competitor, of his cheating on income tax; perhaps this is one reason why he goes to church less willingly than his wife. He feels less at ease there. He feels a little pharisaical in thus publicly parading his piety, for he very well knows what is not right in his real life, and what he does not feel capable of putting right.

Perhaps this is also a reason why in church we see men who are generally less virile, less taken up in life's struggles: civil servants, teachers, men who can more easily lead a life apparently spotless. Like such men, women generally are less conscious of their sins.

He then gives as an example a mother-in-law who is cruelly jealous of a daughter-in-law, yet may convince herself she is acting in love and is a fine Christian!

His statement about a man's knowing "what he does not feel capable of putting right" would certainly be a good explanation of why many Japanese men who accept Christ

182

disappear from the church after a year or so, given the close-knit web of big business and age-old custom in that country. But is Tournier referring to people in the West who are just nominal Christians, or does the same hold true for born-again men? I would hesitate to class them all as "less virile" and as liars and cheats.

Tournier has insight into human nature born of much counseling, but it seems to me that sins like lying, adultery and cheating, because they are, or have been until very recently, regarded by the general public as unethical, may cause a twinge in even a comparatively untender conscience. Such things as jealousy, pride, bad temper, prejudice regarded as principle and so on, require a real meeting with the Lord in humility and love, by both men and women, before they are appreciated for the horrible things they really are. The scribes and Pharisees were men who neglected this, and thus were frequently rebuked by Christ, while women were not (as far as we know from the record of the Gospels).

We can add the views of two rabbis, views which agree with many of the Christian theologians, and also with the pharisaic spirit. Jesus Ben Sirach said, "From woman was the beginning of sin, and because of her we all die," and, "No wickedness comes anywhere near the wickedness of a woman." Philo was more specific: "The woman, being imperfect and depraved by nature, made the beginning of sinning and prevaricating; but the man, as being the more excellent and perfect creature, was the first to set the example of blushing and of being ashamed, and indeed of every good feeling and action." I find it hard to discover in this statement any trace of that masculine trait Tournier speaks of, that is, that "the man is in general more conscious of his sins than the woman is of hers." Philo's conviction seems to have been not so much of his sin but of the greater imperfection and depravity of woman, a view shared by many of his fellow men through the centuries.

Does the Common Pagan View Prove Anything? Donald Guthrie in his comments on 1 Timothy 2:11-15 notes that the equality of the sexes received little recognition in ancient times, mentioning that Greek and Hebrew thought were equally unsympathetic to the idea. He continues,

The entire subjection of women mentioned by Paul relates primarily to public worship as it was then enacted, and reserve must be exercised in deducing universal principles from particular cases. The idea, however, of women's subjection is not only engrained in the conviction of the mass of mankind [which would not of itself be a justification for it, he allows] but also appears to be inherent in the divine constitution of the human race.

Perhaps adding a few illustrations to the ones I have given earlier will help to emphasize the universality of this idea.

Aristotle, for instance, said, "Because all women are worthless, it is better to marry a little bride. She will do less harm than a big bride." Solon, "for the convenience of all conditions of men," listed what was available to them in the way of women in the Greek states. First were wives, who presumably were off limits to other men. They were kept for the purpose of bearing legitimate children, existed for the most part in ignorance and seclusion, and did not even sit at table with their lords. From earliest childhood these women had been allowed "to see as little as possible, hear as little as possible, and inquire as little as possible." Second, were the Hetairai, aliens or freed slaves who could not marry Greek citizens. They were the only free women in Athens, and were often courtesans to male citizens. A few were of outstanding achievement and talent, and scorned marriage because of its enforced ignorance. With little stigma attached they could be unveiled and attend affairs with men whose wives were restricted to the inner house (in some respects quite similar to Japanese men and geisha until recently). It is thought that Damaris was one of these since no other type of woman would be at the Areopagus. Another group were public entertainers, often imported slaves who played the flute and danced at banquets; at the height of these affairs they would often be auctioned off to the highest bidder. Then there were concubines, slaves made members of the household with the knowledge of the wife. Lastly there were prostitutes procured by the state. The revenue from these enriched the public treasury, and so maintaining them was considered "a public-spirited measure." Not one of these situations for women sounds pleasant.

Further east, Siam had a proverb: "Teach a buffalo before a woman." From Hindu gurus we have such statements as "A woman's education should not go beyond the oven" and "A woman's object of worship is her husband."

W. M. Thompson, speaking of the Arabs in *The Land and the Book,* says that such a concept as the woman in Proverbs would be a moral impossibility to an Arab. The men dislike even to mention the women of their household. As examples of their "mildest and least offensive" proverbs about women he gives: "The only religion for a woman is to stay at home." "Everything is easy but women, and the mention of them." Another advises not to let women folk live in the upper story or learn to write; "treat them roughly and accustom them to hear 'No' for 'Yes' will make them insolent." A parting blessing often used by Arabs was,
May the blessings of Allah be upon thee.

May your shadow never grow less.
May all your children be boys and no girls.

This dislike of girl babies seems almost universal, and if men had discovered earlier what produces a boy baby the human race would have been in danger of dying out! As it was, women have often been blamed unmercifully, and divorced, for not bearing sons, although we now know it is the male sperm which determines sex.

For further evidence of the worthlessness with which girl babies have been viewed, consider this letter written in the year 1 B.C. by an Egyptian working in Alexandria to his expectant wife: "If it is a boy, keep it; if a girl expose it." This was a common practice, of course, and it is noteworthy that the early Christians did not expose their children and even began to rescue some who were abandoned.

The value which females were accorded until quite recently in China is well illustrated by Marie Monsen in her book *The Awakening*. She makes the horror stories of present day anti-abortionists seem pale by comparison. Monsen tells how in the early 1920s she and another missionary were teaching some Bible study courses to heathen women. She began to speak about infanticide.

Suddenly, in extreme amazement one of the women said: "Can't we do what we like with our own children?"

We talked about it a little longer. Then they broke down:

"Oh, I have killed three."

"And I five. . . ."

"I took the lives of eight of my children."

"And I of thirteen, but they were all girls."

All of the others had probably been girls, too, and only two out of the 16 women in the class did not confess themselves guilty of this.

Why is this conviction about the inferiority of women, and the fear or contempt with which they have been viewed, "engrained in mankind"? Why do Asians, for instance, believe the *Yin* stands for earth, moon, darkness, evil and the female sex, and the *Yang* for sun, heaven, light, goodness and the male sex? It could be that it is "inherent in the divine constitution of the human race," and I am quite prepared to believe that God in his inscrutable will has ordained it so. Yet as I read some of the Christian commentators' explanations and justifications for this phenomenon, I cannot help but feel that they sound more like the views and attitudes of the rabbinic and pagan worlds than like the words and actions of Jesus Christ.

As I pondered this problem and looked at commentaries on Genesis, I was struck with the words spoken to the serpent, "I will put enmity between thee and the woman" (Gen. 3:15). H. C. Leupold pointed out "the eminent propriety about having the one at whom the devil aimed his attack to be the one from whom his downfall emanates. Furthermore, by leaving open the question of from just which woman the Savior was to be born, God mocks the tempter, always leaving him in uncertainty as to which one would ultimately overthrow him, so that the devil had to live in continual dread."

I had always assumed the devil is more or less omniscient, but I have talked to several ministers recently who say this is not so. Otherwise, he would never have driven Judas to betray Christ and thus bring about the salvation of the world. So it has occurred to me that possibly because of Satan's dread of and hatred for the unknown woman through whom his downfall would come, he may have largely been responsible for the fear, contempt, degradation and rejection to which women have been subjected down through the ages. Even though Christ finally came to vanquish sin and the power of the devil, and placed women in a more favorable light, it has taken nearly two thousand years for this engrained conviction to begin to be erased.

We have noted previously that a Jewish male was taught to thank God daily that he was not born a Gentile, a slave or a woman. With this in mind Paul "asserted that these categories, with their antithetical privileges and priorities characteristic of fallen humanity and maintained by the law were abrogated in Christ" (as the Boldreys suggest). According to most English versions, Paul had declared to the Galatians that "there is neither Jew nor Greek, there is neither bond nor free, there is neither male nor female: for ye are all one in Christ" (Gal. 3:28). The Boldreys point out, however, that "most English translations fail to show the interruption caused by *arsen kai thelu* ('male and female') and thus miss its importance in the text." The series "neither . . . nor" has been interrupted by the use of "and" and the technical terms *male* and *female* (not man and woman) are used, so that it seems to be a direct quote from Genesis 1:27. They suggest the translation should be this:

There is neither Jew nor Greek.
There is neither slave nor free.
There is no "male and female."
For all of you are one in Christ Jesus.

"In other words, in Christ humanity transcends the male/female division. . . . For men and women, this implies the war between the sexes is over."

Thus any discrimination on the ground of being "female" is ended among Christians. True, we are still each individual men and women, with characteristics which will determine our actions at certain times, especially within the family. But the logical conclusion would appear to be that in the Christian community or church, especially, there can be no justifiable discrimination merely on the ground of sex.

If the female sex ever was the more guilty of sin, Christ has now removed that guilt forever. If it was weaker morally and intellectually, he delights to show his strength through such human weakness. He does not regard *woman* as a separate category any more than *slave* or *Gentile*; he sees each person as a redeemed soul, an essential part of his body, the church.

What Is Abrogated by the Gospel?   I finally found one recent commentator who has made on this subject some penetrating observations which deserve to be quoted at length. This is J. Stanley Glen in *Pastoral Problems in 1st Corinthians*. Referring to the tradition of the greater inherent sinfulness of women, which some think is indicated in 1 Timothy 2:14, he notes that both the Old and New Testaments are singularly free from texts derogatory to women, the most likely one in the Old Testament being Leviticus 12 where the birth of a girl baby rates twice as long a period of ceremonial uncleanness as a boy.

L. L. Hastings, however, in *The Wonderful Law*, suggests that this may have been for the purpose of preserving the balance of the sexes by "assuring that the births in families composed mostly of girls would be less frequent than in those in which boys predominated, and that because of this regulation 112 Jewish males were born to every 100 girls." Someone else has concluded that the eighty day period of separation was actually a boon to womanhood and provided a baby girl with a better start in life through a longer period of constant care by the mother—certainly a happy result from a law taken to indicate that greater defilement is caused by girl babies.

The idea of "uncleanness" resulting from childbirth was held by the Roman and Anglican churches until recent times. It appears in the latter's prayer book as the "Churching of Women." Dyson Hague tells us in *Through the Prayer Book* that it was

a quaint survival of a very ancient custom that was common both in the Eastern and Western church, possibly an echo of Old Jewish doctrine and practice. The idea was that the defilement of childbirth prevented a woman from going to church . . . without some sort of purification service. So all through the middle ages an English mother after childbirth came to the door of the church wearing a veil like that worn at confirmation. After several psalms and prayers the priest led her by the hand into the church, chanting in Latin "Enter into the temple of God that thou mayest have eternal life. . . ." The whole service was evidently intended to show the woman was being readmitted to the privileges of the church.

It is hard to see why doing what she was supposed to be created to do should be the means of separating her from the church.

Glen comments,

The conception of the greater sinfulness of women was not, however, incorporated into the theology of late Judaism in a consistent way, and so does not influence the main thrust of its doctrine of sin to any extent. In this respect Paul is not exceptional. His extra-biblical traditions relevant to women were not incorporated into his primary doctrines, even in his thought of Adam in relation to Christ, where contrary to what we might expect, there is not even an allusion to Eve [1 Cor. 15:21-22]. These traditions lie, as it were, alongside his primary doctrines, and alongside his Gospel, unassimilated by them, so that his conception of women, as of slaves, is not essentially challenged.

The problem that emerges concerns the extent to which the subordination of women, even within Paul's Christological interpreta-

tion, is justified. From the evidence reviewed, doubt has been expressed regarding the origin of such subordination, viz., its derivation from extrabiblical tradition. In other words, before the question of the place of women in the church can be answered, we have to answer the prior question of whether we recognize the traditions which were mainly responsible for Paul's view of women. Are these traditions properly regarded as coming from the canon of Scripture? Or if they do come within the canon of Scripture, do they fall within the category of those things which are abrogated by the Gospel? This latter question prompts another—one which makes us conscious that the whole matter of the place of women in the church depends on our doctrine of the Scripture: what are the things abrogated by the Gospel, and how are they abrogated?

A very interesting question indeed! It reminds me again of the apostolic injunction that believers must refrain from blood and things strangled. How and by whom has this been abrogated? Glen goes on to suggest that the issue cannot be evaded, as Calvin tried to, by saying that Paul's words in Galatians 3 refer only to Christ's "spiritual kingdom." Glen thinks Jew and Gentile were meant to be reconciled in their outward relationships as well as in spirit:

The Gospel is a power that shattered and continues to shatter slavery, not only as a spiritual and mental form of bondage, but as an institution. And no less can be expected of that slavery which historically has been of greater scope, and of much more serious and tragic consequences than the formal institution of slavery itself—the subordination of women to men. . . .

What we have to consider, therefore, is whether in a Christological interpretation of the relation between the male and female we should speak of the subordination of the latter at all. For if the subordination is mutual, as Ephesians 5:21 so clearly indicates in its exhortation to be subject the one to the other, we should recognise it. To do otherwise, and on Rabbinic grounds for the sake of maintain-

ing the legalistic authoritarianism of a patriarchal order, is to un-
dercut the Gospel. At this point, of course, most men will find it hard
to surrender the last vestige of masculine pride which this order
sustains, and to see their relation to women governed exclusively
by the Gospel . . . of grace. Their masculine pride, confronted by the
agape of the cross, will perhaps die harder than religious pride,
which is represented by the righteousness of the law.

It takes a man to say that, and no doubt some will consider him a traitor to his sex, but it was a surprise to find
other men with similar views much earlier. Theodore Weld,
assistant to the great evangelist Charles G. Finney, said
more than a century ago, "The devil of dominion over
women will be one of the last that will be cast out" of man.
Seth Cook Rees, one of the founders of the Pilgrim Holiness Church, believed one of the marks of the ideal church
is no distinction as to sex and had his wife as co-pastor.
"Nothing but jealousy, prejudice, bigotry and a stingy love
of bossing in men have prevented woman's public recognition by the church. No church that is acquainted with the
Holy Ghost will object to the public ministry of women" was
his opinion.

If the reasons given by Paul to Timothy for not letting
women teach—that she was born after man and was deceived by Satan—were completely unknown before, then
we would certainly assume that they were a revelation of
God to Paul. If they were repeated elsewhere in Scripture,
that would make a stronger case. But since they are a clear
reference to Rabbinic teaching, it does seem possible the
comment may be of no greater weight to us today than was
Paul's quotation to Titus that "The Cretians are always liars,
evil beasts, slow bellies" (Tit. 1:12-13) and that he should act
accordingly. At least one commentator suggests that in the
Greek the first words of 1 Timothy 3 ("This is a true say-

ing") could belong equally to the end of chapter 2 and no one has found evidence of such a saying about bishops. Chrysostom was also of that opinion.

Where does this leave God's ideal woman? My guess is that she will not be concerned with trying to prove any personal equality with men, although she will be ready to help alleviate known discrimination and hardship to others. I may seem to some to be trying to prove equality in this book, but my aim is rather to indicate that individuals should be judged on their capacities and not their sex. The purpose is really twofold: first, to defend Christianity from the claims made today that it has downgraded women and to show that it is in fact some ecclesiastics and commentators, as well as almost all of paganism, which has done this—not the Founder of the Christian faith nor the general trend of the Scriptures; and second, to find evidence that many great women missionaries were not necessarily out of God's will in evangelizing and preaching.

I think the ideal woman's concern will be, in the spirit of Christ and the words of Paul, "Let each esteem other better than themselves" (Phil. 2:3). She will be aware of her own weakness and tendency to sin and will therefore seek the more to depend on Christ and abide in him. She will with humility seek to glorify Christ and try to make him known by others, since in that same chapter to Timothy Paul says that God wishes all to be saved and come to the truth.

With regard to the ministry of a church (perhaps largely from custom), I think that generally speaking both men and women prefer to listen to a man preach, and his public ministry will normally have a wider impact than a woman's. I do not see how a mother with children, or even most wives could give their time to the twenty-four-hour-a-day duty expected of most ministers. On the other hand, I cannot find in Scripture that that is necessarily the church pattern God had in mind. If a woman has a clear assurance of God's leading and no desire to "lord it over" anyone, it seems difficult to deny the validity of an audible ministry for her in Christian gatherings and in personal witness, since God himself has chosen to use many women in this way as the next chapter, and missionary history, reveal.

The later rabbis taught it would "lower the honor of the congregation" to have a woman read the Scriptures in the synagogue although provision had been made for it in the early days. But does it necessarily lower God's honor? Certainly woman was first to sin, but Christ has now offered himself the full sacrifice for all sin. There is no need for a temple building or priesthood. Paul said to *all* believers, "Your body is the temple of the Holy Ghost. . . . Ye are not your own, ye are bought with a price: therefore glorify God in your body, and in your spirit, which are God's" (1 Cor. 6:19-20). Also, "Ye are the temple of the living God; as God hath said, I will dwell in them and walk in them" (2 Cor. 6:16). Verse 18 of the same chapter makes it quite clear that this is addressed to both women and men.

Once one has grasped this amazing and humbling truth that hour by hour our body is the temple of God, then a man-built church on the day of the Lord does not seem quite the awesome place a human priesthood would like us to believe. That good bishop may feel that woman's temperament is earthy and unsuitable in church, but whatever we once were, however weak and however deep in sin, God assures us: "Ye are washed . . . ye are sanctified . . . ye are justified in the name of the Lord Jesus" (1 Cor. 6:11). He deigns to make us his temple, holy, "perfect through my comeliness which I have put upon thee, said the Lord God" (Ezek. 16:14).

14
WOMEN WITH A MINISTRY IN THE EPISTLES

Having considered at length the role to which Paul may or may not have intended to restrict women, we will now look at some women mentioned by name in the Epistles who were obviously more than benchwarmers.

Remarkably, most of these references occur in Paul's greatest doctrinal document, his letter to the Christians at Rome. This important theological statement about sin and salvation addressed to believers in the prestigious capital city was entrusted to a woman named Phoebe, who carried it the several hundred miles from Corinth to Rome—an arduous, even dangerous journey in those days. And some consider this "a responsibility only given to someone of official standing."

Phoebe In the Greek text Phoebe is called a *diakonos*, a word which appears twenty-two times in the New Testament. In eighteen places the AV translators render it "minister" and three times "deacon," but for Phoebe they change it to "servant." Some of the newer translations have put "deaconess," but the Boldreys point out that this is misleading because the separate office of deaconess was not established until the fourth century, long after Phoebe's death. They claim that in the early church both men and women were deacons, and "the grammar of the word does not even distinguish between 'deacon' and 'deaconess.' "

In introducing Phoebe to the believers in Rome Paul says that he wants them to "receive her in the Lord, as becometh saints, and that ye assist her in whatsoever business she hath need of you: for she has been a succourer of many, and of myself also" (Rom. 16:2). Many have imagined from this that she must just have given him hospitality, done his laundry and possibly run a soup kitchen, and that she needed a little cash for this. But actually the word translated "succourer" in the AV and "helper" in other versions is the feminine form of *prostates* (Latin *patronus*), "the title of a citizen in Athens who took charge of the interests of clients, and persons without civic rights." It literally meant "one who stands before, a front rank man, a chief, leader of a party, protector or champion," according to Liddell and Scott's lexicon. Phoebe was therefore obviously a woman of means and position and may have acted as Paul's "patron." He was therefore asking the men and women believers in Rome to "stand by" her, to be at her disposal in any way she required, since she had "stood forth" as a leader or supervisor. It is the same kind of consideration he asks for other church leaders and elders in 1 Thessalonians 5:12-13 and 1 Timothy 5:17.

With the thought of Phoebe as a deacon in mind, let us look at 1 Timothy 3:1-12, where Paul is advising Timothy on the kind of people he should (or should not) appoint to positions of leadership in the church. He refers first to overseers ("bishops" in the AV), deacons and women ("wives" in the AV). I, like many other people, because of this translation imagined Paul to be referring to the wives of the overseers and deacons. Hendriksen states, however, *That these women are not the wives of the deacons, nor all the adult women of the congregation is clear from the syntax: "The overseers therefore must be . . . ; deacons similarly [must be] . . . women similarly [must be]. . . ." One and the same verb (i.e., "must be") co-ordinates the three, the overseers, the deacons, and women. Hence these women are here viewed as rendering special service in the church, as do the elders and deacons. They are a group by themselves.*

Hendriksen does not see these women as constituting an "office of the church," endowed with equal authority with men deacons, but rather as "servants or assistants" who perform ministries "for which women are better adapted." Like most commentators, he does not specify what these might be. The early church held that the women deacons of 1 Timothy 3:11 introduced women to the overseer, assisted in the baptism of women and visited the women's part of the homes.

Father Jean Daniélou, in his *Ministry of Women in the Early Church*, also agrees with this. He assumes that baptism was by immersion, that the whole of the body was anointed with oil before the ceremony and that for women candidates this had to be done by a deaconess. (A priest might only anoint the head where women were concerned.) He quotes the rule of an early monastic order, which states, "When she who is baptized comes out of the water, the Deaconess shall receive her, instruct her, and look after her, to the end that the unbreakable seal of baptism may be impressed on her with purity and holiness." He tells us there was an Ordination of Deaconesses in the Eastern church, the *Apostolic Canons* giving the following instructions:

Thou shalt lay thy hands upon her in the presence of the Presbyters, the Deacons, and the Deaconesses, saying, "Thou who didst fill Deborah, Hannah and Huldah with the Holy Spirit, thou who in the Temple didst appoint women to keep the holy doors, look upon thy servant chosen for the ministry, and give to her the Holy Spirit that she might worthily perform the office committed unto her."

Canon 15 of the Council of Chalcedon added that "a woman may not be ordained under 40 years of age." However, there does not appear to have been complete agreement about this ordination of deaconesses, the Council of Orange (441) decreeing that "deaconesses should not be in any way ordained." The problem was finally resolved when deaconesses were absorbed into the nunneries. The order was suppressed in the Latin church in the sixth century, not until the twelfth century in the Greek church.

Modern theologians are just as divided on their views of Phoebe and these other women. Ryrie tells us that Lightfoot and Godet both think Phoebe had an official ecclesiastical office; but, although he agrees that *prostates* does imply official ruling, he maintains "there is not a single instance of a woman holding such an office (unless Phoebe herself be the single instance, but such an exception from the Bible would be strange in view of the fact that there is no extra-Biblical exception)." He then rather unconvincingly says, "The writing of 1 Timothy was not many years after that of Romans, which fact (if it be true there were no deaconesses in Romans) does not help the argument that these women were deacons."

In A.D. 112, however, a secular source did speak about women deacons. Pliny the Younger wrote to the Emperor

Trajan, who had recently appointed him governor of the province of Bithynia, and asked for advice about whether he should persecute Christians, since he knew little about them and the "contagious superstition" was spreading in every age, class and sex in city and countryside.

I thought it the more necessary to inquire into the real truth of the matter by subjecting to torture two female slaves who were called "deacons," but I found nothing more than a perverse superstition which went beyond all bounds. Therefore I deferred further enquiry in order to apply to you for a ruling . . . because of the number of those who were accused. For many of every age, every class, and of both sexes are being accused.

Why did Pliny choose these female slaves as the ones to torture? Was it because they were least important, hardly regarded as human, or because he thought they could be made to talk more easily? I think it sounds as if Pliny really wanted to know what this Christianity was, and so chose these two because they held some kind of official position and therefore would know most accurately. Ryrie, however, thinks it would be "risky" to use this evidence to prove the existence of a female diaconate: "It would be very difficult to prove that these women acted in any officially designated capacity." It is equally difficult to imagine Pliny using the term if it did not mean anything.

As for women weakly giving way under torture, the opposite was often true. A number of cases are recorded, but one must suffice here. During the severe persecution of Christians in the Rhone valley mention is made of a slave girl called Blandina. F. F. Bruce tells us,

Others feared least her physical frailty might not be equal to the torture. In the event she showed herself such a noble confessor her example strengthened all the others; her tormentors exhausted themselves in their attempts to make her renounce Christ. "I am a Chris-

tian," was her steadfast reply; "and there is no wickedness among us."

Another hint that possibly women held an official position is found in 1 Timothy 5:1-2, which reads, "Rebuke not an elder [literally, *presbyter*] but intreat him as a father, . . . the elder women [presbyteresses] as mothers." W. K. Brown takes the term as indicative of office, Bishop Ellicott and many others as merely referring to age. However, the fact that the office of presbyteress was abolished by the Council of Laodicea in A.D. 363 indicates that at some period prior to that there must have been such a ministry.

There is also the possibility of a special order of widows, as indicated in 1 Timothy 5:9-12.

Women in Rome We return now to Romans 16, where after his commendation of Phoebe Paul sends greetings to a list of people evidently well-known to him. No one today knows for certain how the church at Rome was started, but it has been assumed by many that since some of the visitors to Jerusalem at Pentecost were from Rome they returned to the great capital of the empire with the message of the gospel. Obviously there was always much travel to and from Rome by business and civic leaders, and evidently some of Paul's converts and acquaintances from his missionary journeys were now there. Of the twenty-six people listed, eight are women, which is rather surprising.

At the head of the list is Prisca, followed by her husband, Aquila. When this couple is first mentioned in the Scriptures, the husband's name comes first; and some have reasoned that because on four later occasions the order is reversed this indicates Prisca's greater prominence in the work. Paul, by the way, usually refers to her by the more formal Prisca, Luke by the diminutive Priscilla.

The AV's rather weak translation of the word Paul uses to describe them is "helpers" (Rom. 16:3). The same word is applied elsewhere to Timothy (Rom. 16:21 and 1 Thess. 3:2) and to Luke (Philem. 24). It means literally "fellow-workers in Christ Jesus" and "signifies they were professional evangelists and teachers" (Adolf von Harnack). As we have seen in Acts, Luke records how they taught Apollos, leading him into the full Christian truth. Chrysostom, in his paraphrase of Acts 18:26, omits Aquila's name entirely, mentioning Prisca alone as the teacher of Apollos. Even Ryrie admits that "it would be difficult to prove that the 'helping' did not include public teaching, and even possibly missionary work."

Paul says not only that they both risked their necks to save his life, but that "all the Gentile churches owe them a great debt," indicating a wide spiritual ministry. In Rome, as formerly in Ephesus, a church met in their home. This has now been excavated under the ancient Church of St. Prisca, and indicates she came from an aristocratic Roman family.

Tertullian, in spite of his devastating accusation of women, also wrote, "By the holy Prisca the Gospel is preached." There are various scraps of evidence in the early records of the church of Prisca's well-known, acceptable ministry in Rome, and some writings known as *Acts of St. Prisca* were extant until the tenth century.

At least five theologians believe that Prisca wrote the letter to the Hebrews. They offer the following reasons to support this view: (1) The letter is anonymous. The name of a woman might have prejudiced its acceptance. (2) She was known to be an illustrious teacher. Much of what is said in Hebrews might well have been said to Apollos. (3) She had close associations with Paul and Timothy, as the author of

Hebrews obviously had. (4) At the time of its writing Paul seems to be dead, and in his last known letter he had specifically mentioned Timothy, Priscilla and Aquila. (5) The author seems closely identified with the readers of the letter (Ephesians seeming to fit best) and hopes to return to them. (6) In the list of heroes of the faith several women are mentioned. (7) There are a number of practical references to both childhood and parenthood. (8) The letter contains the theme of pilgrimage ("Here have we no continuing city" 13:14) as if the writer had personal experience of this. Four nautical terms are mentioned in the Greek, although these are not all apparent in the English translation, and Prisca made at least four sea voyages. (9) Hebrews shows a great interest in the tabernacle, natural if the author and her husband were tent and leather makers. (10) Sometimes the author's voice is in plural form, which might indicate the inclusion of Aquila. R. Hoppin in *Priscilla: Author of the Epistle to the Hebrews* adds further evidence gleaned from Qumran, the excavations in the catacombs at Rome and second- and third-century writings which make this theory seem a strong possibility. Probably, though, we shall have to wait until we get to heaven to know for certain who wrote this letter.

Others in Paul's list at the end of Romans are "Mary who has worked hard for you"; Narcissus, who seems to be the head of a household; Tryphena and Tryphosa, a cute sounding couple whose names mean "Dainty" and "Delicate," who may have been twins and who certainly were "workers in the Lord"; and "the beloved Persis" who had also "worked hard in the Lord" (NASB). Then there is Julia, about whom we are told nothing; and two whose names are not given: the mother of Rufus "and mine," and the sister of Nereus.

One of the most intriguing names is in verse 7: "Salute Andronicus and Junia, my kinsmen, and my fellowprisoners, who are of note among the apostles, who also were in Christ before me." The AV has the name in the feminine with which the majority of ancient commentators agree, but newer versions have put it in the masculine, Junias (perhaps because the translators felt from some of Paul's restrictions on women that it ought to be a man?). The problem is caused by the phrase "who are of note among the apostles." I had always assumed that this meant these two people were known to the twelve. This is not how the early church viewed them, however. Chrysostom wrote, "Oh, how great the devotion of this woman, that she should be accounted worthy of the appelation of 'apostle.' "

The meaning of the word *apostle* is "one sent forth." It was first used by Jesus in sending out the Twelve—"It had reference to the particular mission, not the 12 men." In Acts it is the ordinary name for the Eleven, but denotes not a restricted office but their worldwide missionary service.

The Eleven always regarded Matthias as making up the Twelve, not Paul, we are told, but Paul continually claims to be an apostle. He seems also to apply the term to Apollos, Silvanus, Timothy, Barnabas and the Lord's brother James. He also refers to "false apostles" in 2 Corinthians 11:13, and obviously people would know at once that these were not any of the Twelve. Lambert concludes,

The true differentiation of the New Testament apostleship lay in the missionary calling implied in the name, and all whose lives were devoted to this vocation, and who could prove by the issues of their labors that God's spirit was working through them for the conversion of Jew and Gentile were regarded and described as apostles.

Charles Hodge agrees that the word means "messengers to the churches," but feels the word has a fixed meaning (that is, it is restricted to the Twelve) and is never used in Paul's writings except "in its strict official sense." In the Didache, however, written about A.D. 100-120, the title is applied to the whole class of missionaries who did not settle in any one church; and there obviously is a little tension developing between these and the local church leaders:

But concerning the apostles and prophets, you are to act thus according to the ordinances of the Gospel. Let every apostle, when he comes to you, be received as the Lord; but he shall not remain more than a single day, or (at the most) a second; if he remains three days he is a false prophet. And when he departs, let the apostle receive nothing but bread.

So we must take our choice whether we regard Junia as the wife of Andronicus and a fellow missionary with him (possibly among those who believed at Pentecost since they were believers before Paul) or else as a man.

Women in Other Epistles Turning to 1 Corinthians, we hear of Chloe. She was probably a wealthy and important member of that church who felt she should send a report to Paul about some of the disturbing things going on there (1 Cor. 1:11). In Philemon Paul addresses Apphia, Philemon's wife. This couple also had a church in their home, as did Lydia and Nympha, the only one of the church at Colossae whom Paul mentions by name in his greeting (Col. 4:15). The AV mistakenly has her name in the masculine. The "true yoke fellow" mentioned in Philippians is thought by many to be Lydia since early in the letter Paul addresses those who fellowshiped with him in the gospel "from the first day"; and of course Lydia and other women at the river were the first converts in Philippi. Euodia and Syntyche (Phil. 4:2) may have done some evangelistic work since Paul describes them as "those women which laboured [struggled] with me in the gospel... with other my fellowlabourers."

In Paul's second letter to Timothy, written from Rome, he says, "Eubulus greeteth thee, and Pudens, and Linus, and Claudia, and all the brethren" (4:21). Who was this Claudia? No one is certain, but E. M. Blaiklock in *The Century of the New Testament* has this to say:

Who were Pudens and Claudia whom Paul mentions as prominent members of the church in Rome? Were they the Pudens and Claudia mentioned in the epigrams of Martial twenty years later? Martial's Pudens was a centurian of distinction, Claudia was a British Princess, and Pudens' wife. An inscription in Chichester [England] tells how a piece of land was presented by one Pudens to the British chief Claudius Cogidubnus, Aulus Plautius' ally. Was this the same Pudens, later influenced by his commander's wife?

Surprisingly, the non-Jewish harlot, Rahab, is mentioned in two epistles, Hebrews and James, being commended in the first for her faith and in the second for her action which demonstrated her faith. The word *harlot* did not necessarily have the same connotation for the Jew as for us today. The New Berkeley Version has a footnote on the Levite's concubine saying, "Deserting her bed and board [and returning to her parental home!] was sometimes reason for the designation 'harlot.'" Jeremias also notes that rabbinic teaching was that "the harlot of Leviticus 21:7 refers only to a female proselyte or a freed bondwoman, or to one (Israelite by birth) that suffered connexion of the nature of fornication." Only a proselyte girl who was converted before the age of three years and one day might marry a priest, since the Jews assumed that all Gentile women and girls would practice prostitution and "so on principle assumed that no Gentile knew his own father."

Lastly, there is the second letter of John, which is written to "the elect lady." Many commentators assume that an apostle would hardly bother to write to a woman and that since the church has been called the "bride" of Christ John was actually writing to a local church and its members. But it is the whole church which is the "bride," not each local group. Nowhere else in Scripture is this term "elect lady" used, however, and furthermore the opening sentence here is almost exactly parallel to that in John's third letter addressed to a man named Gaius. (Compare "The elder unto the elect lady [Kuria] and her children, whom I love in the truth," 2 John 1, and "The elder unto the wellbeloved Gaius, whom I love in the truth," 3 John 1.) J. Sidlow Baxter says, "Some would have us believe that this lady and her children were really a church and its members; but verses 5, 10, and 12 convince us such an idea is far-fetched and artificial. We are glad that at least one little epistle in our New Testament is addressed to a Christian *mother*."

All these women, and what is said about them, may seem few and insignificant in comparison to Peter and Paul and their important work. There is no doubt that the majority of full-time Christian workers have been, and probably always will be, men. There is actually more said about a number of these women, however, than about the majority of the Twelve, most of whom are not mentioned by name after the resurrection. Considering the Jewish teaching on women, the prevailing customs of the day and the record of most other religions, these many references are indeed remarkable. These women obviously enjoyed Paul's and John's respect and warm appreciation. They were not merely silent benchwarmers but hard workers for the church, the gospel and the Lord. They have been followed through the centuries by many other sisters in the faith who have heard God's call to Christian service.

REFERENCES

Adeney, Walter F. *Women of the New Testament*. London: James Nesbit, 1901.

Barackman, Paul F. *Proclaiming the New Testament: The Epistles to Timothy and Titus*. Grand Rapids: Baker Book House, 1964.

Barclay, William. *Daily Study Bible: Letters to Timothy, Titus and Philemon*. Philadelphia: Westminster Press, 1956.

Baxter, J. Sidlow. *Explore the Book*. Grand Rapids: Zondervan, 1960.

Birnie, W. S. *The Search for the Twelve Apostles*. Wheaton, Ill.: Tyndale House, 1973.

Blaiklock, E. M. *The Century of the New Testament*. Downers Grove, Ill.: InterVarsity Press, 1962.

Boldrey, Dick and Joyce. "Woman in Paul's Life." *Trinity Studies*, Vol. 22, 1972.

Brow, Robert. *Religion: Origins and Ideas*. Downers Grove, Ill.: InterVarsity Press, 1966.

Bruce, F. F. *The Growing Day*. London: Paternoster Press, 1951.

_____. *New International Commentary on the New Testament: Acts of the Apostles*. Grand Rapids: Eerdmans, 1951.

Cohen, A. *Everyman's Talmud*. New York: E. P. Dutton, 1949.

Daniélou, Father Jean, S. J. *The Ministry of Women in the Early Church*. Trans. Glyn Simon. London: The Faith Press, 1961.

Edersheim, Alfred. *The Life and Times of Jesus the Messiah*. Grand Rapids: Eerdmans, 1965 (orig. 1886).

Evening, Margaret. *Who Walk Alone*. Downers Grove, Ill.: InterVarsity Press, 1974.

Fitzmyer, J. V. "Features of Qumram Angelology and Angels of 1 Corinthians." *New Testament Studies*. Cambridge: The University Press, 1957.

Glen, J. Stanley. *Pastoral Problems in 1 Corinthians*. Philadelphia: Westminster Press, 1964.

Guthrie, Donald. *New Testament Introduction*. Downers Grove, Ill.: InterVarsity Press, 1971.

_____. *The Pastoral Epistles*. Grand Rapids: Eerdmans, 1957.

Hague, Dyson. *Through the Prayer Book*. London: Longman, Green and Company, 1932.

Hastings, James, ed. *The Greater Men and Women of the Bible*. Edinburgh, 1915. Quoted by Ryrie.

Hendriksen, William. *New Testament Commentary, 1 and 2 Timothy and Titus*. Grand Rapids: Baker Book House, 1957.

Héring, Jean. *First Epistle of Paul to the Corinthians*. Trans. A. W. Heathcote. London: Epworth Press, 1962.

Hiebert, D. E. "The Apostle Paul: Women's Friend." *The Christian Reader*, June-July 1973.

Hunt, Gladys. *Ms. Means Myself.* Grand Rapids: Zondervan, 1972.

Hurley, James B. "Did Paul Require Veils or the Silence of Women?" *Westminster Theological Journal,* Vol. 35, No. 2, 1973.

Jeremias, Joachim. *Jerusalem in the Time of Jesus.* Trans. S. H. and C. H. Cave. London: SCM Press, 1969.

Lambert, L. C. "Apostles." *International Standard Bible Encyclopedia.* Chicago: Howard Severance Co., 1915.

Lange, J. P. *Genesis: A Commentary on the Holy Scripture.* New York: Scribners and Son, 1868.

Leupold, H. C. *Exposition of Genesis.* Grand Rapids: Baker Book House, 1942.

Little, Paul. *How to Give Away Your Faith.* Downers Grove, Ill.: InterVarsity Press, 1966.

Lock, Walter. *International Critical and Exegetical Commentary: Pastoral Epistles.* Edinburgh: T. T. Clark, 1924.

Luce, H. K. *Cambridge Greek New Testament for Schools and Colleges: St. Luke.* Cambridge: The University Press, 1949.

McNally, Jane A. "The Place of Woman in the New Testament Church." Unpublished master's thesis, Wheaton College, 1944.

McPheeters, Julian. *Proclaiming the New Testament: The Epistles to the Corinthians.* Grand Rapids: Baker Book House, 1964.

Money, John. "Biological Imperatives." *Time*, January 8, 1973.

Monsen, Marie. *The Awakening.* London: CIM, 1961.

Morgan, G. Campbell. *The Corinthian Letters of Paul.* London: Charles Higham Son, 1947.

Narramore, Clyde. *A Woman's World.* Grand Rapids: Zondervan, 1963.

Phillips, J. B. *Ring of Truth: A Translator's Testimony.* London: Hodder and Stoughton, 1967.

Poppin, Ruth. *Priscilla: Author of the Epistle to the Hebrews.* Jericho, N.Y.: Exposition Press, 1969.

Pulpit Commentary. Vols. 19 and 21. Ed. H. D. M. Spence and Joseph F. Exell. Grand Rapids: Eerdmans, 1950.

Ramm, Bernard. A critique of an article by Nancy Hardesty. *Eternity,* January 1971.

Ramsey, Sir William. *Cities of St. Paul.* New York: A. C. Armstrong and Son, 1908.

Ryrie, Charles C. *The Place of Women in the Church.* Chicago: Moody Press, 1968.

The Sacred Scriptures of the Japanese. Trans. Post Wheeler. London: George Allen and Unwin, 1952.

Sayers, Dorothy. *Are Women Human?* Downers Grove, Ill.: InterVarsity Press, 1971.

Shedd, Charles W. *Letters to Karen.* Nashville: Abingdon, 1965.

Strachan, James. *The Captivity and the Pastoral Epistles.* New York: Fleming Revell, n.d.

Tournier, Paul. *To Understand Each Other.* Richmond: John Knox Press, 1962.

Vos, Howard F., ed. *Religions in a Changing World.* Chicago: Moody Press, 1959.

Wilson, Dorothy Clarke. *Lone Woman.* Boston: Little, Brown Co., 1970.

Wright, Fred H. *Manners and Customs of Bible Lands.* Chicago: Moody Press, 1953.